Fingerprints of Time
Jerry Smith

Xavi and Xena Publishing – Rock Hill, SC
ISBN 978-0-692-07537-1
Library of Congress Control Number: (pending)
Title: Fingerprints of Time | Jerry Smith
Digital distribution, 2018.
Paperback edition, 2018

Dedication

To late Miss Lucille Collins, she was my inspiration.

CRACK COCAINE

Something that should not have ever been conceived under humanity's sun; a robber of lives and extinguisher of souls. You have even stolen the embryo in the womb that has never seen the moon. A republic even declared a war against you, and you are still breathing, who supports you. When you have cause so much shame you don't even have a passport, but your footprints are around the globe, how did you learn so different dialects. Nothing good has ever come from you, but the mind cannot resist your taste. Generations have vanished because of your touch; the landscapes of time are painted with granite pillow cases, because of mortals spending time with a coca leaf, what a tragedy.

I WONDER IF DEATH HAS A GHETTO

Watery eyes continue to litter the milky, broken spirits vanish each day. Poverty holds nations hostage for generation, and humanity acts like he can't see them. The voiceless know that they have no value, the societies that they hibernate in has shown them that. The sun smiles on creation and ask for nothing in return. While the rain thinks that it's an honor to quench our thirst, I wonder if death has a ghetto. Why does this inhuman atmosphere continue to flourish, and we and we all get our breath from a Goddess. Every heartbeat that sees the moon is going to expire, that's why ghettos should never live. There is no compassion for the have nots, even though they did not create their conditions.

The little beautiful innocent roses born into this nightmare is going to be handicapped. Just take a good picture of the crumbling infrastructure of the human existences.

I wonder if death has a ghetto, because all, I see growing around me is misery. Will the same spirits rule the republic there?

VOICELESS

There is a nation suffering inside another nation, they were kidnapped from a continent two and a half centuries ago. Their offspring have become zombies, addicts, inmates and hopeless, while decaying on the outside.

Spirits are playing with the wind, stars can still see them trying to look through, blue irises that can't feel them. Pigmentation is knocking on shores doors wanting to know, if love blooms there for brown voices. Clouds are waiting to carry broken lives to another galaxy, were they have a chance to be valuable. The sun informed the hopeless that, the Milky Way did not need them in its republic anymore.

While the moon apologized for humanity, standing over there acting like he can't see, the demise of a race of human beings.

WHERE IS GOD

I hibernate in the Milky Way where spirits have lost their faith. Anarchy owns cities on all the continents, ideology has forgotten how to comfort. A pandemic is blooming in the wind and war is, sins only friend. The sun continues to be horrified by, what it has seen for centuries. Where is God, the embryos have been euthanized in the cocoon for decades, and no one can hear them ask why. Nuclear weapons fly, mankind has invested too much time in them not to try. Generations are growing in destitution, while drinking from the cups of bitterness. Heartbeats are being taught that their, is pleasure in death.

WHO IS GOD

A manuscript that they said was inspired by you has found my spirit. I love how you reminisce about being sisters and brothers in the family of humanity. But very few seeds that you planted here can hear, their hearts have too many colors and the angels that they have been following only destroys. You can't see their inside from where, I am, you once said that, what goes inside a man does not defile him. It's what comes out but, can you see what is being inhaled and injected in your garden of Eden. Multitudes of souls have expired and been enslaved by pharmaceuticals that never sleep. The Lord's prayer should help the finite minds see because only you can hear the grave speak. Your voice is stronger than gravity, silenter than a butterfly's breath waiting, on us to reach for the light. Death has never seen your kingdom and sin doesn't have the directions to it love is the only way to find it.

VICTIMS

Eyes pretend that they can't see the roses withering in the concrete sea. A voyage to mars have more value, than them breathing, the rainforest teardrops are leaving. A shooting star can flee a chanceless galaxy, but the destitute will never, vanish from the western hemisphere.

Their heartbeats have been suffering in this system for more than three hundred moons. lending currency to other countries, even comes before them, depression is always near. Imported narcotics are breathing where they hibernate; being trapped since birth means that you will never heal. Homicides are flouring across the plains, the same pigmentation is the blame, extinction is the end of the game.

DEAR FATHER

And not just in word a strong man of very few words with the insight of Plato and a heart feel with love. But he never knew how to display it, because he was never shown hugs,

You taught me how to hunt with a weapon of steel with a Leopold scope attacked to it, looking for tracks that may disappear. Then angling with him along the catawba river that leads to the sea, a fish pulling on the line can't wait to see it. You taught me how to view the world around we and to watch out for snares set for me. I have witness you rise for decades and going out to provide for your D.N.A in every way. In this culture of discontent were storms continue and eyes wish to be free, you are my best friend thank you for guiding me.

AIDS CHILDREN

Flowers that have inherited a curse, blooming on earth, rain often falls from eyes; medication hangs around. An endless stream of misery and suffering runs through your veins but remember you didn't sin. In this land of ends, I don't know why the creator let this happen to you but always smile underneath these Red, White, and Blue clouds. Where things aren't always what they seem to be, water flows deep down inside of me for thee. the earth trembles under my feet, flowers fall from the tree of life so will we, stars flee the night, always know my heart weep for you even when, I am not breathing anymore. Don't let this curse hurt your breath even though it may be cold. Whatever time you may have reach for the stars and hold your head up high never asking why. A lot of you will never have a queen or king in this land of doubt, where there are scientist trying to find a way out.

BLACK MALES

The hourglass is nearly empty your species is becoming extinct on this road call history. You have become a burden on society one out three of you passed by, on the continent has a record and it's not playing on the radio. Black males you have transformed from being called king and prince to inmates and felons, being transplanted across North America. To hibernate in Federal castle of concrete and steel owned by investors, now there is no place for you in their culture. 'The Andromeda Galaxy should be the next destination, you cannot be shown that you aren't wanted anymore, then you have been shown in the milky way. Four hundred years of servitude has destroyed the black males spirit, living in a stolen nation dream.

BROTHERHOOD OF NATIONS

It's pass time for mankind to sit down at the table of love and figure out the reason for their ignorance. Because for the infinite time, that man's shadow is upon the earth he should live in harmony with other ideology. The battlefields of time are fill with crimes, against humanity along with the brains that won't abhor anymore. Eyes that won't covet anymore, hearts that won't beat any longer, lungs that don't need oxygen anymore, ears that can't be deceived anymore and arms that can't hug anymore. Noses that won't smell anymore, hands that won't clap anymore, legs that can't stand anymore and feet that won't follow any longer. Mouths that won't speak with a fork tongues any farther and fingers that love pulling triggers anymore. Souls that can't thirst anymore and voices that don't hurt human beings any longer.

BISHOP
Perry Huitt

A faithful spirit that rises before the sun and puts his will last for the kingdom to come. He rides the wind North, South, East, and West to harvest souls, from times of old that have never been hold. The gifts that the lord has bestowed upon his prophet are blooming in our sight. Wisdom flows from him like the Nile River runs through time, nourishing the Lord's garden of life, while there is still light. His faithfulness is wider than the sky, warmer than the sun, that never ask for anything in return. Gentle like a baby slumbering in the night, brighter than a star twinkling in your eyes.

MRS AUSTIN
My Algebra Teacher

A radiant spirit that wants to see humanity succeed and is giving her intellect to achieve it. She travels across the Milky Way, massaging minds with algebraic expressions. That coordinate pupil's destiny into the educational galaxy, where hope dwells. Variables may come often, and integers may invade dreams. All that, Mrs. Austin wants is for her pupils, to keep believing. She is an inspiration to me; I follow her guidance, like a star in the night. It sure has made my life bright, and I appreciate her.

THE GRAVEYARD

The final stop under these cirrus clouds were storms end and granite pillows with names become best friends, dirt knows no sin. Love ones come often, water flows free from deep down inside of we, voices speaking beautiful metaphor that visit from the soul. Eyes looking into heaven as if it's just another door wondering if they will see you anymore. Flowers being placed to decorate the site, hearts can never say goodbye. Dreams of you come late at night my hands reach out for you, wishing that they could hold you tight.

U

I saw what you did to a people that couldn't see and that was before they found a star to tell them where they are.

They never found joy that is in each other's heart-considering they never had a start.

Trying to run away but never getting far, trapped underneath all these stars.

Old dust, I often wonder if you have any fun. So many people come from you and often returned unharmed.

They live life most of them of little charm and often born to families that teach them to harm.

It must make you sad to see that your offspring can do such things to one another, as if they are not seen.

They have come up with colors that help them hate one another.

So when they return to you dressed in their fine clothes and wrapped in a tree, will you teach them to love and see?

IMAGINE

There is no emperor with congress to spend the wealth of the empire on galactic research and warfare. While the peasants starve, and anarchy takes charge of the fifty stars with his colleague hopelessness. No concrete jungles to hold the adolescences hostage, while desperados with prescription pads and thugs selling crack, poisons the population.

Imagine that there was never a virus developed to attack the immune system. A civilization that never learned racism that has contributed to its demise. No petroleum to die for, that is hibernating in Mesopotamia were the Tigris and Euphrates rivers touch. Imagine that humanity didn't fail, and addictions are just nightmares coming to steal our serenity. I no longer covet heaven or fear hades the light that, I have been searching for is not in this land of the expiring.

DRUGS CIVILIZATION

The western hemisphere is the stage, addicted spirits decorate the landscape like a Christmas tree. Foreign plants and chemicals applied for citizenship, because they said that they have been illegal immigrants for decades. Their D.N.A is appearing in toxicology reports and in patients across the continent. Domestic and foreign concrete pharmacists are at war with each other, over control of the territory to distribute pollutants. The empire has fallen, an illusion is holding it up and poverty owns the population. Hopelessness rises each morning in their eyes, like the sun smiling in the east, and lays its head to rest in the west.

NEFERTARI

A rose that bloomed in the Middle East around a multitude of thorns, but the west can't see. Her heart hears metaphors that the sun doesn't believe on its journey across the sea. War is all that her pupils have witness since birth, bombs raining from the night sky, has taken away trust. The wind said they came from the western hemisphere, passing by him, while he was crossing the Atlantic. Falling to the earth, leaving it crying and extinguishing generations, making sure they never grow. Time transplanted the rose to the west, with scars and memories of her, decease family tree. Cultivating an attack that satellites will receive, trying to satisfy a deity that millions read about, but no one has ever seen.

REV. ULYSSES G COLLINS AND ANNIE COLLINS

A love that blooms once every millennium in a galaxy, two souls knitted together by the hands of God. For a purpose that's only known by his will to be done leading his servants across the stars to harvest lost sheep for his kingdom to come. The eternal course that they have chosen is decorated with glory look at how God is blessing their life. As they continue to walk towards his light, nourishing souls that trials have turn cold. The faithfulness that they have to each other is one to behold. The ring wrapped around their left finger will never grow old.

FORGIVING A REPUBLIC

North America is the stage, importing spirit is the trade, a five thousand mile kidnapping starts the blame. Red hearts, blue eyes, and white lies decorate the landscapes of minds. The brutalized voices are still echoing through time wanting to know if their will ever be reparations for the crimes, against humanity committed on them. If only the sun would testify, maybe the culprit's offspring wouldn't say that, they aren't responsible for, what their forefathers controlled. The wind can even be a witness to all the tears, that he hears falling from the eyes of souls. That has cross the Atlantic Ocean, naked and fettered together in the belly of a ship. Now the republic wants their relatives to forgive, and to have amnesia.

BORN A SLAVE

Why does the sun rise, when there is no joy in my eyes just the site of misery decorating the horizon? Ragged clothes wrapped around my abused body, I wish that my bare feet could deliver me from tomorrow. Hunger visits me often, but mama said that it's going to be alright, it doesn't hurt that much late at night. The cabin that we hibernate in sits on dust, two straw pallets one in the corner the other by the door.

Daylight always meets at the cotton field my fingertips are raw, the cotton bulbs have small thorns in the top, I pray you never get to touch. I once ask mama where papa was, she said that she didn't know, master sold him many springs ago. Servitude was born with me, it doesn't take eyes to see that this shouldn't exist.

CHICAGO

The blood of your slain, cries out from the dust and the wind doesn't want to be associated with you anymore. Teardrops continue to flood your streets, and mothers' whys, are knocking on heaven's door. Bullets are taking breath around the clock; hopeless fingerprints can never be stopped. Depravity is flourishing across the square miles, justice is trying to hide. Martial-law may have to help citizens groom their adolescents before anarchy caress them, The Statue of Liberty is embarrassed about what she sees; the residents are breathing in fear where they sleep. Because the outlaws have taken over the avenues, so please little children don't you cry, Osiris won't let all of us expire.

MARTYRDOM

I have seen my last shooting star, running past the moon on my journey to paradise. Invaders have appeared on our shores, winds from the west have delivered a mighty adversary. Bring with them instruments of mass destruction, that their hearts enjoy using. They have committed atrocities all around through history on other continents, just as the sun. Never forget they used a biological weapon to steal a continent, extinguishing millions of natives and enslaving a race. Now you understand what, I taste in this Milky Way of waste were spirits thirst for oil. Ideology and faith consumes my soul, the love for my country, brothers and sisters keeps me warm. If my breath must leave me for them to be free, then let it be.

REPARATIONS

Close your ears you mayn't want to hear about, what has been hurting the sun for three centuries. North America is the stage tragedies decorate the days, crimes against humanity leads the way. The Atlantic Ocean is the main highway and the mayflower knows the way, it has been carrying the victimize from Africa to the east coast in forty days. To a fate that only a criminal mind could conceive in this land of death. Breeding farms are growing flesh, they are being auctioned off, Mother are mourning, masters need more slaves by May the cotton fields are dormant. Millions of the victimize have return to the dust never knowing their family tree, name religion or where they came from. Only the wind can answer there in eternity.

FRENCHELL

A rose that blooms once in a lifetime, with starry eyes that hypnotized my mind, and a heart that's worth more than a diamond mine. My eyes miss your sunny smile that that keeps my spirit warm, when you aren't around. While walking, I often hear your voice only to turn around, and it's a bird sing a love song, that my ears hold dear. Frenchell when, I was alone you were there for me, you never left me alone because you cared for me, and you are sure appreciated.

If you ever get lonely, deep down in your heart, late at night while laying in the dark. Just look out your window at the moon and stars, you will know that, we are closer than you think we are. Time and death will never take us apart, because our souls are sown together for infinity.

MY DAUGHTER IS A HEROIN ADDICTED

The truth has been knocking on the door of my heart. The little princess that the creator gave me, soul is torn apart. I could never imagine that a poppy plant would, steal her heart, while traveling down a high school hallway. The love of her life is a syringe, spoon and belt, they spend their nights together feeling for a vein. That flows away from the Milky Way, her dreams never getting to reminisce about the pass, a needle took her class. My eyes saying how, I feel about you, the wind saying that it will never forget you in the eulogy. Heaven forgive her woes, the ride on the spoon you never want to know. Tomorrow will never get to see you, a belt has memories of you.

The ocean didn't have a clue, teardrops wet her casket, when will it be the last of it.

LYNCHED

A South Carolina oak tree can tell you about a rope hanging from it. On a cold October night in 1916 with eight hundred eyes cheering, and two hundred tongues lying about a spirit swing in the wind. Because it wanted humanity to show him respect as a human being in this land of white supremacy. Where one drop of black blood has been suffering for four hundred years, dripping with fear. Heartbeats born into illiteracy and afraid of the moon, because they know that terrorizing will come out to slay soon. Unmarked gravesites litter history, voices often reminisce about them.

Teardrops continually try to find them, but the dirt is too ashamed to reveal where they hibernate.

MARTIN LUTHER KING JR.

A prophet that was annihilated because he wanted to see the offspring of slaves to be treated humanely. His lectures echoes across the milky way but have fallen on a deaf republic. If his eyes could return from the dust they would be appalled at the condition of the have nots. His plea to the greatest empire the world has ever seen means nothing., The suffering of a nation inside a nation is a tragedy.

Mental illness, alcoholism, drug abuse, aids and incarceration are the only statistics that the offspring of slaves are flourishing in. This a result of having no value in a republic for eternity, without a voice or hope.

MOTHER TERESA

A radiant saint sent by God into this ocean of suffering and expiring to hold the hearts of the destitute.

She heard a voice from beyond the stars, inside a call telling her about squalor that will be seen in tomorrow.

Calcutta is the garden of sorrow under the rule of another empire and the native have no value. Mother Teresa an instrument of God's love, her eyes have never said no to the epidemics that surround the globe. Stooped and a mere five feet tall and draped in a white-and-blue sari, her palms are not afraid to caress. The aids infected flowers before they are laid down to rest. She captured the Nobel Peace prize, she said, I accept it the name of the poor, God has not call me to be successful only to be faithful. We have had the honor to have a true humanitarian breathing in our mist feel with compassion and selflessness, you are surely cherished.

TO THE UNBORN SEEDS

If, I have return to the dust before you open your eyes, remember to adore your life and always think positive. Underneath this Red sun, White snow, and Blue ocean, where it mayn't be so bright. I've lived through the wilderness of the shadows of death and witness the plagues riding by, at times, I haven't been so proud. Wearing the scars and tattoos from my trials and tribulations as, I view the future that's waiting on you. To the unborn seeds as long as you are breathing keep believing because, I know you can achieve. Reach out to education, it will lead you to a University and Doctrine degree, just wait and see. You may be responsible for building a new humanity.

CRAZY HORSE

Born free and rise in desperation, he once road the plains like the four winds and witness the buffalo disappear like the snow vanishing into the earth. He often saw treaties broken like leaves falling from a tree. His clean heart became like a stone when he thinks of all the broken promises to the tribes and seeing his people, blood flowing like a stream heading for the sea. He finally realized that the Indian nation was vanishing like the sitting sun and their tears falling from their eyes like rain out of the clouds, because they have no land. Along the path of time Crazy horse cross path with Sitting Bull and their journey took them to, the little Big horn valley for a date with the seventh cavalry. They set up tepees beside the Big Horn river, with about eight thousand souls trying to find peace, after fleeing the reservations of genocide. That December morning the seventh cavalry riding with death in their hearts headed for Sitting Bull camp. Crazy horse and the braves went out to expire with them. After about a thirty minutes battle, Long knives Spirits and a few braves decorated the landscape.

The seven cavalry was annihilated, Crazy horse flew into the black hills like an eagle trying to find freedom. But the only freedom he found was beside Wounded Knee creek six feet deep.

MY BROTHER IS A DRUG ADDICT

Crack cocaine knocks on the door of his soul, he answers it and the spirit moved in. Letting all of his dreams go, sitting there holding his breath with a glass pipe touching his lips. Sweat running down his face as if he's in a race, crystals decorate the plate. Eyes popping out if he has seen a ghost, captivating mind tells him he needs more. Heart beating fifty miles an hour, headed for Hades, a foreign realm. The architect that build, crack cocaine should have never been born, that way the globe wouldn't have all these addicted souls.

ROCK HILL ADULT EDUCATION

Coming to you is the best decision that I have ever made in my life because my life wasn't so bright. The smiling eyes that greet me each day lift my spirits to new heights and the encouraging words make my heart stop. The professionalism that the teachers have is something to behold. Making sure that the pupils achieve their goals, in the educational world, where there are opportunities that keep growing. For the staff to hold themselves to such high standards, they must have a wonderful director, and that is, Ms. Sandy Andrews. She has refined the Rock Hill Adult Education Program, it is a success and you are surely appreciated.

Poet – Jerry Smith
5-17-17

KRISTI

The sun that rises in my heart and rest in my soul a spirit, I am so grateful that the creator let me hold. I couldn't have a more beautiful queen blooming in my life, with angel arms that hold me tight. While we are lying here in the night looking out the window at the moon wondering in the sky, while a shooting star pass by. My wanting ears love hearing your sweet voice in the morning it sounds like a bird sing a love song. Kristi thank you for walking with me underneath this endless blue sky, you are my dream come true. Each morning that I rise, I look forward to seeing your charming smile, and those light brown eyes. When rainy days visit my way, you even know the words to say to make the clouds obey. My spirit is filled with joy knowing that you love me with all your might. And if, I owned the four seasons you could any of them that you need, because that's how much your gentle soul means to me.

THE FALL OF A CONTINENT

The Milky Way is the stage and you can't choose your D.N.A, fate leads the way. Scuba diving gear can give you away if your flippers don't have anywhere to play. A vessel knows the way to paradise all you have to do is to get out of the way.

Remember only two can stay, heartbeats racing passing shooting stars to the date. The republic is warring away, conquering is the only thing to quench its thirst. The citizens are uprising, there has been domestic violence, the king came on satellite for an hour. Speaking words that have no value, seventy percent of the spirits believe that things are going to get deplorable. Militias are gathering on the horizon there is no more faith in the flag, they think that soon it will only be the past.

I LOVE

Seeing the sun smiling each morning in my life feel the wind whispering through time. While watching the flowers blooming in the springtime. Listening to the birds sing their tones, while smelling the honeysuckles all of the time. I love witnessing the lighting bug light up the night time, as the moon sits by gazing at a shooting star turning into a wish. Walking beside the ocean thinking about mankind, and will they always be blind. I love all of the hunting memories that hibernate in my heart that comes out when there are storms. Angling the silver lakes of time, casting lures into the underwater world, looking for a feeling.

TRAIL OF TEARS

There is no need to follow the star just track the sound of teardrops falling from destitute eyes. As they stagger west, expiring along the days ahead to the reservation of death. The conquered tribes journey began two thousand moons ago in homicidal minds that thirst for their land along the Catawba River were their tipis hibernate.

Winter lead the way, with his best friend snow covering the plains. The blankets that wrapped around their shivering bodies had a fever that crossed the Atlantic Ocean on a ship. Oklahoma could never rescue them, it would be the place where their bones, could rest for eternity.

LOVENESS

Born on a continent of pain, waking up every morning to shame. Her hair looks like a hornets' nest. Her frail frame hibernates in a hut with a straw roof and the bed is the dirt floor. The stream that quenches their thirst is stocked with parasites with the Ebola River as its source and the mortality rate is rising. Malnutrition is there to stay, Loveness has no energy to play. Primates are the delicacy for today, yellow eyes and bare feet paint her way. Aids carried her mother away last May. Stars shine where we pray, dark clouds cry over the hearts that never got to see this day, what will be the tribes fate?

MY PEOPLE

I wish that, I was not me so that, I could not see all this pain inside of we, there are twenty four hours in a day and we don't mean a second here today. My brother's life mine and my life is theirs and life is what's it's all about and we have never got what we deserved so life is very hard to figure out. But things are not what they seem and who we are is not the blame, and one day we must die, remember brother, I won't cry. Is it my fault, what I feel is this life the way we live? Tell me softly why you hate, wake them up before it's too late, help my people dry their, tears help erase these five hundred years, if only people could take thing back and love the things they have attacked.

My heart is hard like a hill, but can someone save us and try to understand the way we feel? Are we here just to survive and can we get through life alive? My people's life is mine and my life is theirs, can I be a bait to fish you out of the path that's in your way, if only you would stop and listen to what, I have to say. This great ocean of darkness has blinded you on your way, only to cast away everything you have to say, tongue-tied along the way; you must not be here to stay. Others have died by this way, let's change continents today.

I FORGIVE
Alexander the Great

Before, I met thee my eyes watched the pyramids rise, while sailing the Nile and my grandfather is the architect of the valley of the kings. The sphinx first came alive in my mother's uncle's mind, as the sun smiles from where it hides. Monotheism took his first steps here without any help, now its offspring are breathing all around the globe. I study at the greatest library known to man before it was stolen, mummification began here. Astronomy is how some of our architecture structures are laid out, take a look at Orion's belt. Moses even flourished in Pharaohs palaces after being harvested from the Nile by a princess and became a patriarch. Jesus took refuge here after an angel awaken his guardian during the night and told him that herod wanted to destroy his light; The afterlife was first conceived in Egypt with his best friend humanity.

GONE TOO SOON

Love has dried up, summer turns to winter, the blooms are falling from the tree of life, light has given way to darkness. Jewels cease to sparkle and gold has lost its charm, the sun moved to Andromeda while the moon walked away. All of our stars expired in the sixties, clouds don't weep anymore, laughter forgot its voice. Smiles never come around and the wind found another galaxy, shadows won't follow, the republics eyes close for eternity.

Souls are hollow and hearts don't thunder, minds are tired of wondering. Arms can't hold the truth, hands don't know why, feet can't travel and the body is no longer a tomb.

XAVI and XENA
My Two Granddaughters

Two roses blooming in the milky way with eyes brighter than shooting stars, running from the night. Their heartbeats are stronger than the wind and my love for them will never end. The sun will always be their friend as they journey through the garden of life. Where there are gifts waiting on them as they follow the educational road. That leads to college degrees that will help them achieve their goals. My two Granddaughters remember to always watch out for snakes, and keep your eyes on yalls father's heart. Because he will always love and wonder how y'all are underneath this Carolina blue sky.

ADULTERY

Before, I committed to thee the sun adored me, smiling in my soul from times of old. The wind us to follow me wherever I wondered until I forfeited my only tomorrows. My Queen vanished along the way and raindrops fall from my eyes to often to say. Adultery can you hear me from here, because if not for you, I would not be drowning in my years.

There is not a vest to protect my mind from the river of regret that flows through it. Knowing that, I have lost the only real love that, I would ever feel for eternity.

A DYING REPUBLIC

Conceived forty degrees longitude, eighty degrees latitude born in fourteen ninety two. Underneath Red, White and Blue stars to capitalist parents with no heart. On this continent, where the Ten Commandments are discarded and a native culture has been extinguished. The incarceration rate is flourishing, stockpiled with the descendents of slaves. That have became a burden to the republic and infinite minds, act as if they don't know why. Epidemics own property in every state, hopelessness, often comes out to stay. Civil disobedience is blooming in a multitude of souls, whose eyes have grown cold from viewing the globe.

X

Since you return to the dust the winters of discontent has grown, the blood that you shed for the seeds that you love so much has yet to be heard. The breath that you gave, couldn't dry the tears of time that fall from many hearts You often spoke of an exodus because you knew that it wasn't enough room, for us in this muddy stream of time. You, you laid your light down that we may see, not knowing that it was never to be. Pharaoh heard you crying out from your abyss, inquiring about your descendants being dismissed so that they won't continue to populate his dungeons, of concrete and steel with their existences. If you can hear me from here things aren't what they seem to be, storms come often and we are still not free.

WHY IS THEIR SUFFERING

When desire is driving your heart and it goes by expectations castle to pick them up, suffering enters into mortals' blood stream. Once it is in the D.N.A it speaks to the mind about the attachments; it hibernates with from times of cold. Which holds the spirit captive in this land where everyone returns to the dirt, after illness has ran its course.

The eyes have lead the soul astray, every since their first date and want is in every breath humanity takes. Greed is the Mother of lust, that why it hurts so much in this whirlwind of covetous.

HUNTING

Dad and I are following a path that leads to a feeling in the meadow. A seven millimeter magnum walks with me, dad enjoys squeezing a browning three hundred magnum, the hunting season is cherishing, I wish that you could see, the sun smiling over the tops of the pine trees, while the earth has snow visiting it. To really feel free with the wind blowing through my mind gives me peace on the inside. As I look down the mountainside, listening to birds singing. Squirrels are dancing across the earth's floors a sound comes from the right Doe's are crossing the creek. Dad and, I are waiting on the bucks to join the show, trees are still holding snow.

TUPAC SHAKUR

A rebel rose that grew from concrete, whose voice is mightier than the wind. Even time didn't know that it wouldn't have an end, in this galaxy of sin. His adolescent bright eyes, could comprehend the poverty that they were trapped in since birth. The Black Panthers tried to quench their thirst, but the emperor sent out his henchmen to extinguish, the only hope. Being destitute didn't destroy his spirit, it only gave him, metaphors to articulate the flaws in the Bill of Rights. On his odyssey across minds that are living in hopelessness, and will never taste freedom. Not knowing that, all that he has is a quarter of a century to breathe, in this ocean of casualties.

SLAVERY HAS NEVER ENDED

The fetters have moved from the wrist and ankles to the mind. The landscapes of North America are witness to, many crimes against humanity the victimized continue to wither. Souls that lost their names three centuries ago, crossing the Atlantic Ocean, in belly of a vessel. Legions of the patriarch offspring are deteriorating in dungeons of concrete and steel that will only destroy wills. Generations of unborn seeds conceived to a fate of hopelessness and destitute. That will never be able to bloom in this Red, White, and Blue soil Voices reaching up to the heavens, searching for a deity to deliver, them from bondage.

THE GRAY HOUND BUS STATION

We meet again after another attempt at forever, and all my expectations blew away in the wind. Finally, I feel the end, the cargo is laid to rest in the belly of the large silver craft with windows all around that plants hearts across the continent. I will never view the longhorn state again leaving behind a voice that, I wish that, I had never felt. The regretful memories will decorate the graveyard of my mind for eternity and haunt me in my dreams. Sometimes, I just would like to wake up and this has been only a nightmare not reality.

FEED THE CHILDREN

It's not a race only a hungry sunrise that won't wait, children that don't know how to play, stomach crying during the day. Being lured to sleep early because there's nothing to quench their taste, poverty knows where they hibernate. Sifting through garbage dumps for decades trying to find nourishments to stop the cravings before it's too much hate. Feed the children it's already too late, thousands close their eyelids last night and didn't awake, what a unnatural fate. The sun smiles on all faith, water quenches our thirst and we all get breath from a woman on earth.

CIVIL RIGHTS

Never got to know me remember, I was never allow to hear, my eyes only witness stars being extinguished. On this Red, White and Blue hemisphere where my voice and dreams disappeared.

Servitude is the only thing waiting on our offspring as they are breathing in misery and drowning in despair. This republic has no vision for them that way we will soon be extinct. History is a witness to our demise he was in the room when humanity was crying. There is no need for a eulogy because the constitution wasn't born to protect me. My slave name is listed under property, if only the wind would take our hand and lead us to another solar system.

Where our D.N.A can flourish without conquers devouring our spirits.

I WAS

Born before welfare in a culture were hearts didn't care, a
century after the light bulb, but there was no light in our lives.
There were no projects, only shotgun houses fill with
emptiness. No restroom only a outhouse, don't fall through,
because there would be no rest for you. No running water to
carry us through, just a creek and candlelight to help us from
being too sad or blue. No father to warm our lonely souls,
only the old coal heater that sits in the middle of the
splintered up floor Mama is disable but fill with love, praying
for four children that she couldn't hold, on these cruel South
Carolina shores. Then one honeysuckle smelling day, a tiny
old lady with a angel spirit and Cherokee smile came to
hibernate with us.

If not for her all that, I would be is a negative statistic.

DYING

The four seasons have no value, and regret rises with the sun each morning. No fruitful relationship ever bloomed for me in the western hemisphere. There aren't any seed to carry on my slave name. It makes my heart smile to know that, I didn't bring another mortal into a life of servitude. That is waiting on them in this, capitalistic society where they will never find liberty. I have been knocking on the door of ideology for half a century, but no deity has answered. Leaving me with a scared up soul on this journey of hopelessness were the stars keeps all the secrets. I no longer fear dying because, living in this system, I am already deceased.

THE EMPIRE IS UNDER GOD JUDGEMENT

The ten billion year old Sun's rays are harmful to the inhabitants, lesions are decorating their body. Flood have swallowed up countries drowning livestock and washing away dreams. Fires burning across the plains consuming structures that hands have crafted and the ground keep aborting her nourishments. Earthquakes enjoy shaking the West Coast, tectonic plates are out of bate. Tornadoes love walking across the Atlantic Ocean to visit the empire seasonally, drink the water at your own risk. Epidemics are breathing in every state, participating in war around the globe won't let you sleep. Anarchy lives on the street, the wealth of the empire goes to erecting penitentiaries. The wind is carrying the prayers of faithful to God; they are begging to be evacuated out of misery.

ABUSED

Can't forget about yesterday and don't want to breathe tomorrow. The raindrops visit my eyes often, along this road called life. Where trespassers should think thrice. Stars rule the night and storms often while unfaithfulness runs free. A loving companionship doesn't bloom anymore in the Milky Way, greed has taken its place. Hearts have learned only to want, what taste good to the mind at the time. My spirit yearns to share dreams with a soulmate before the wind stops blowing in my lungs. Traveling through time, passing by windows from times of old seeing faces that, I wish weren't cold.

NAT TURNER

A light that was born a slave on the continent of North America, that can never be extinguish. Where homicides come often and racism lives free, the pilgrims never allowed them to learn to read. Cotton fields will not always be in our dreams, eyes wondering if the twill ever feel healing. The wind can't tell us what hears, voices reaching out for ears, history won't repent.

Hearts beating looking for a brighter day, teardrops falling from spirits along the way. Fingerprints are giving upon liberty, because she has help destroy them. Death is the only freedom that our feet will ever see.

BORN IN HARM

The Milky Way is the stage, deceitful emperors decorate the continents. While the natives are withering, and their offspring is growing destitute. The empires spend their wealth on instruments of destruction and wars. Research means more than the poor hearts, that's why civilization is falling apart. Chemical dependency is stealing spirits just listen to the cemetery, you can hear them. A pandemic has traveled the globe, scientist has found its deoxyribonucleic acid behind a multitude of doors. Famine continue to rob bodies of, human rights, I wonder why humanity won't put up a fight. Ideology has ran its course, when will the deity make his approach, the disciples souls are losing hope.

CONCRETE MEMORIES

Why bring me memories, only to leave me swimming in the ocean of a lost humanity feeling for reality. Trying to satisfy a taste, crossing many faiths on my odyssey through the Milky Way. Taboos invade my sight, some even recite the Bill of Rights on the road to contrite, will mortals ever see the light. Time can you see, your landscape littered with wandering spirits living lives they didn't choose. Mental illness often comes out to stay, unattainable goals leads the way to empty places. Fingers of time can't continue to covet other doors, two percent of the empire, owns all the minerals.

WHEN I DIE

Let my smoke be a signal in the sky, sprinkle my ashes by the seaside, remember mother don't you cry. Tell my seeds that, I said good-bye and that, I will see them on the other side. Remind the homies to stop doing drive bys, little Neeshas mama still cries.

Please help dry the raindrops, that fall from the little children's eyes tell them that, I have lived a dusty life under this unforgiving republic. Where at times it is hard to smile let them know that there are ill gotten games that will help their life fail. The Gestapo's that are planted in the ghettos lead to the dungeons of steel so beware.

There are already enough flowers growing there, with broken hearts and washed out dreams. Adolescents let your itching ears feel me, you are from where the pyramids speak, and the sphinx guards your life.

I LOVE YOU

I am glad, I got to love someone in my existence and that's you. If not for you, I wouldn't have this feeling, every second that my heartbeats it's looking for you. The sun has warmed a multitude of souls along this journey call life. But we are the first to be married by it mother earth wants to be your maid of honor and angels said they are going to be bridesmaids. Destiny said that he is waiting to walk you up the aisle a star ask to be the ring bearer, while the wind is looking forward to taking us on our honeymoon. The moon told me that, I was always to be the groom and roses, lilies they volunteered just to appear. My ancestors from Andromeda are coming Sagittarius said he may come alone sometime, I wonder. The sky said that you know that he will be there, aunt snow said she couldn't make it. Your relatives from Jupiter said that they wouldn't miss it for the world and a hummingbird wants to sing two hymns. June said that he would love to be the anniversary and the creator said that it would be an honor to be the best man. He has a colleague coming with him eternity.

LOVING YOU

It gives my heart something to do as it walks across Saturn headed for eternity. Your gorgeous eyebrows, and lashes leads your way, those light brown eyes brightens my days. A kiss from your sweet cherry lips takes my breath away, know that you are in my soul to stay. As my fingertips find their way through, your satin black hair. My ears desire to hear the hypnotizing words from your caring voice that nourishes my spirit. I look forward to seeing your smile in the sunlight, and late at night seeing two stars twinkling in your eyes. The ocean blue sky is on our side, it's a pleasure to feel your fingerprints on my heart, and our dreams carrying on.

HIROSHIMA

Little boy sleeping in the belly of a big iron bird, he does not know where he is going. Born in North America and wean in the desert you have many researchers, nurturing you there. The fortress that holds you so dear, knows that you will soon disappear, into the atmosphere. The iron birds path has been chosen, it must glide at thirty two thousand feet above the earth's floor, so that it can't be seen.

Course set for the Far East, where the sun awakes from its sleep. After arriving over the site, little boy is ready to light up the night, for hundreds of miles, spirits will not breathe anymore. For decades trees won't bloom and generations will come, go, but history can never let go.

DIVINE LOVE

It existed before breath and it can't be taken away because you don't have wealth. You aren't chosen by race or the continent where you hibernate, gold can't capture it and death won't end it. Sin can't beguile it because, it needs nothing from the flesh. Divine love will walk with you through this valley were everything expires. It will inspire your heart when it is disappointed and guide your life when there is no light. Quench a thirst when the Milky Way dries up, warm souls after the winters of discontent, by bring eternal life with it.

JOHN THE BAPTIST

A light breathing in the wilderness and living example of faith, giving baptisms to everyone that believes in the scriptures. Never having a earthly adobe or suit to wear his body wrapped in camels hair. His vocabulary paints the path to salvation in the valley of death. Lips have never touched fermenting grapes, eyes have seen something that has no end. His ears heard a voice calling from beyond the wind.

EVERY OTHER SIXTY-SECONDS

A flower return to the dust on the continent of Africa, she receives them all with open arms. The rain that runs down her face for them is warm, but we must remember that this earth is not our home. The pain from the indigenous sacerates the soil, but it's already spoiled, and the sun lives high above showing love. While the wind comes by and carries us alone, memories will always have a home, I often think about why there is wrong. Many eyes never get to wish on a fleeing star, I wonder where they are and the moon stands there with nothing to say, he remembers their birthday.

WILL YOU MARRY ME

My heart loves you and my dreams never want to be without you. The sun enjoys smiling on your angel face, as the wind whispers that it is a pleasure to hear your charming voice. My skin looks forward to your celestial touch. The stars come out at night just to see, themselves twinkling in your hypnotizing eyes. Mother earth gives us her blessings and father time said that he would always be kind. While the moon sends his congratulation and said that he would see us soon. Two souls, love for one another blooming in eternity.

NEVER STOP DOING WHAT YOU LOVE

One day the sun is going to open its eye and you won't view it, the days will continue but you won't be here to feel them. The trials and tribulations that have touched your life, have no sting anymore, that door has been closed for eternity. Hold on to the wind coming by, birds sing lullabies, and the moon smiling in the night. Maybe even catch a ride on a shooting star if your heart is bright.

The years disappear like a vapor, so cherish them they won't wait for you. Never put anyone joy before yours, because that's all you really have in this world.

DIVORCE

Two hearts that fell out of love with each other, while spinning on a rock in the Milky Way. Minds to walk out on souls, never to return to pick up verbs that the adolescents shouldn't have heard. Leaving their spirits to wonder the globe with no faith to hold. Only washed out dreams that control the atmosphere, that they are drowning in. Divorce robber of memories that decorate the future that won't be there for them. Voices that rain tears, will only remember the wind whispering the existences of lost. Faces erased from hearts for eternity, what a tragedy to see the family tree vanishing.

MARY
Mother of Jesus

A divine vessel, the to be artificial inseminated two millenniums ago and the carnal minds still wonder how.
Entrusted with the only hope for mankind, if they would take the time to read the sign. She is in front of the sun, standing on the moon in intercessory prayer for a humanity that's wounded. Preparing for the crucifixion at a place called Golgotha, a name that will echo through time. Mary kneeling at the foot of the cross, eyes overflowing with raindrops, heart broken by fear, watching her son's breath disappear.

JESUS OF NAZARETH

The first to be conceived artificially into a world that could not see, bring lyrics that lead to eternity. He often reminisce about a dimension that eyes can't see, you can only visit spiritually. He loves us so much, just take the time to comprehend the sermon on the plains it can heal humanity.

Seeing him walking on water isn't hard to believe, he just wants us to know that the laws of nature doesn't apply to him. So when the storms are raging down in the soul and gale winds toss the spirit, we have someone to go to in faith to console them.

MY PSYCHOLOGIST

Stronger than the wind whispering in time, she's carrying my burden from deep down inside my mind. I tried to run away but never getting far surrounded by all these Red, White, and, Blue flaws. It has been decades, since addition found its way into my veins, now it's hard to wean them out of my stream. Wanting to talk about things, that wants to remain blind, that has held my family tree hostage in the Western hemisphere. Traumatized by racism that owns the society, little negro boys, tears have nowhere to hide in it.

Learning that the back door would only let me in, two water fountains one fill with sin. The bathroom have their own names, I must remember, which one apply to me; my skin will help me see. Having to run away from voices that hate we, carrying scars that can't be seen. Dear mama bless her heart is disable and the sixties are deadly.

THE SPIRIT OF GOD

Free like the wind, quieter than the twinkling of an eye, faster than light, brighter than the moon, smiling in the night. Older than the earth, that hold us in her arms, wider than the universe that will never harm. Smarter than prophecy, stronger gravity cleaner than water, gentler than a butterfly, dancing in time, deeper than the black hole, that has no crowns. Farther than tomorrow is from an expired life, closer than a whisper is coming from your esophagus, hotter than the sun would be, if you could hold it in your palms. Colder than Antarctica is, on a moonless night, loves us more than, our minds can comprehend. Sweeter than honey, that is born inside the tree; came into the world, so that we may see.

NOTHING LAST FOREVER

The daylight gives way to the night, the four winds came by, but didn't tarry long. The four seasons even takes turns, and the stars ran away from the night, while leaves abandon the trees. Rivers and streams dried up, clouds drift away, the rain came by but never stays. Snow often visits, for about three days then disappears, thunder and lightning came by, but they had somewhere else to be. The hail usually drops in but, I have not seen them in a mouth, the glaciers are vanishing in Alaska. The beautiful flowers even expire, my love has moved out, of my heart. Names are lost forever, voices will not be heard again, eyes closed for eternity.

Time has a strange way of turning thing to dust like we must.

KINYADA

You are the love that rises in my heart every morning and my wish upon a shooting star. When dreams visit me, you are with them, every since you have been, blooming in my life my thought are bright. Rainy days come often, but they only help my love for you grow, under this china moon. Kinyada, I have never believed in miracles, until know, the journey that my soul has been on for eternity came to an end. When you said that you would be my, Nubian queen. I look forward to riding with you in my chariot, into the wind, passing by the pyramids that have no end. While watching the sunset, melt into your smiling eyes, with your sweet lips against mine.

DEAR POOR CHILDREN

Lets baptize our tear stain faces, we occupied many continents and dates. Dreaming of sleeping away but never seeing far, trapped underneath all these stars. The Sun blooms each morning, yet our stomachs aches from loneliness there is so much beauty in this world, but we taste emptiness. The moon smiles on every soul, and ask for nothing in return, and we still yearn for concern. Dear Poor Children don't you cry, butterflies live in cocoons before they fly keep your broken eyes toward the endless sky. Where the stars is the keeper of the night, knowing that the winds of prophecy will soon ride by.

There is a creator that gives and takes all day he invented the rhythm of our heartbeats. Why we were the have nots is beyond my comprehension, because all of you are precious little angels, so always smile for me.

BORN A HAVE NOT

Born on negro universe, gazing at cotton stars shooting past hopeless eyes, wishes falling from broken hearts. Planted on Plantation Boulevard, watered by the tears of sorrow, and cool by the winds of bitterness. Suffering in the hands of humanity, toss by the waves of loneliness, While drinking from the wells of despair. The earthquakes in time has separated us for eternity, abandon by grace, minds looking for another date. Reminiscing about the climates of discontent, wondering if they will ever past. Waking up underneath these same palms of harm daydreaming about when the savior will be born.

WARS

A plague in the minds of time tomorrows nightmare in today's eyes, family members are clothed in black standing around weeping. The earth parts itself accepting coffins like seeds, love ones whisper the eulogy from the expired life. Words that echoes from deep down in hearts, knowing that they won't always be apart. Memories of them aren't that far off, especially as we sleep underneath all these
stars. Empires will rise and pause the citizens should not always be pawns. Time and death for sure will take us apart, but it should not be because of a dictator's thirst for oil.

SUICIDE

Lingers in my cerebellum continually, as regret knocks on the door of my heart repeatedly. Disappointment follows all of my dreams, on this odyssey call life. Expectations travel through my bloodstream, only to vanish into eternity because the flesh cannot fulfill them. Wants bloom across the plains every second that a breath is taken. My eyes can't keep on raining in a failing culture, ideology is preached often and anarchy runs free. It's time to see, what is after this capitalist thirst, because there will always be mortals cursed. My soul is tired of being incarcerated in this tomb called a body.

MY IVORY QUEEN

Silky gold hair touching her hips, those Carolina blue eyes brightens my days. Lips sweeter than strawberries that, I can't wait to taste, my ivory queen comes out to play, that angel voice is never too late. The fragrance that possesses her body has my heart held hostage and it never wants to be freed. Your love is like the wind even though I don't see you, I can still feel you. Because in your caring arms is the only place that my soul desires to exist.

YOUR LOVE IS

Deeper than outer space, wider than the galaxies, taller than the black hole, stronger than the four winds blowing in my mind. Closer than the stars, twinkling in a groom's eyes, warm as the sun smiling in time. Late night visitor in tomorrow's dreams, calmer than a dove under humanities wings. Pure as a baby heart slumbering in time, hard as a diamond in a brides mind. Sweeter than honey to the souls taste, gentler than a butterfly floating in the atmosphere.

WATER

The quencher of my thirst, you once covered the entire globe only to recede back into the dust. The life source of all flourishing things, flowing millions of centuries, carving streams in hearts that have never been seen. Baptizing souls from times of noble, washing the minds of all beings with wondering eyes, so it seems. While the swan sings more beautifully of events soon to be.

CARRYING REGRETFUL MEMORIES

Time often plays back pictures into my mind, reminiscing about trespasses that were unkind. Eyes raining enough water to flood a town, heartbeats reaching for an endless love. Seasons have tattooed my soul cold, while waiting on judgment day. Dreams no longer visit my spirit anymore the sun, showed me that they don't come true. The moonlight comes often to guide me through, shooting stars are fleeing the milky way maybe, I should too.

THE HOLOCAUST

Time has walked away from many faces and places, born North, South, East, and West in this milky way of unrest. Eyes close for eternity never to grow, ashes from the fiery furnaces, falling from the sky like snow. Minds knocking on humanity's door, seeking compassion for the spirits that have not shown. Time needs to know, that mortals can't continue down this path, eyes are tired of overflowing. The memories we continue to hear, has our hearts trapped in fear. Prayers go up, I wonder if the creator can see, all the broken families that will never be.

PRISON CONTINENT

Eighty degrees west longitude forty degrees north latitude the Atlantic Ocean has touched many hearts along the road of life. Concrete and steel fortresses populate the landscapes holding wretched souls that time has no use for. Judge by a republic that has broken every law known to humanity in the pursuit of conquest. Polluted by addictions and lead by covetness, satellites decorate the night sky, research means more than the poor children's cries. Dying dreams fill their poverty stricken eyes, the wind can't even hear the mothers whys.

SABRINA AND COURTNEY

Two angels sent by God to be a blessing in all our hearts, carrying smiles that could charm the stars. My precious daughters, I will always wonder how yall are. For now time has taken us apart, but as sure as the sun warms our love, and the moon watches over us while we slumber, we will be together again after this tour. Yall are two of the most beautiful princesses a father could have so always be courageous and proud. I wish that I were there with yall, to be a umbrella when it rains a sled when it snows, your coats when yall are cold, and shelter in times of old. My love for my daughters is wider than the sky, deeper than the ocean, stronger than the wind, and brighter than the sun that has no end. I miss my two princesses more than the night would miss the stars.

MY HOOD

Come take a look through my eyes sure wish that, I was born blind, the adolescence wear red flags on their body. Street pharmacists decorates the corners, there is a artist, but no one has seen his face, the hieroglyphics he paint live on pyramids around the way. Harlots walk the paths in the moonlight, dealing flesh as a way of surviving in Hades and they are being found slain; no one knows their trick.

Gunshots ring out like its thunder it makes me wonder who eyes a mother won't see in the morning. My hood where all the homies are relocating to the dust, while the other ones are retiring behind concrete and rust. Becoming extinct is the only category that we are leading in around the Milky Way.

HOPE

Do you know your way to the Milky Way, nations have been displaced. Hearts lost faith, tyrants rule the decades, wars often come out to stay. Orphans decorate the landscapes of time carrying loneliness inside their souls while blooming in insanity. Hope can you hear me from where you hibernate before, I expire, I have something to say. The global population is living in hopelessness and mass incarceration litter the Western hemisphere. While the poverty rate arid pandemics are flourishing in a declining galaxy.

VIETNAM

A land where foreign names are hibernating, for eternity underneath a yellow sky with three red clouds. Rubber trees grow tall along the Mekong river delta, just open your mind and see. Monsoons come daily, locust with steel bodies fly often, fills with eyes watching, you can smell the napalm burning. Harmful hands with lustful hearts came from the north, bring with them wretch souls. A gold star wrapped in red, fell in the south, peasants trying to runaway but never getting far, trapped underneath this hopeless cause. Cannabis and poppy plants bloom all alone, military minds are thinking about transporting them home.

HOW WOULD YOU FEEL

If your mama was a prostitute, and gave breath to you in the ghetto. Where you never knew who your father was, wandering around in this concrete jungle where predators kill. How would you feel if you often fall asleep at night with a empty stomach and eyes filled with raindrops, no mama near with other siblings in fear. How would you feel if your blood, started to run with thing in the night. Then caught a bid in the castle of rust and steel, that never heals underneath these Red, White, and Blue scars.

How would you feel if you found love, in your life and didn't know how to give it back, because you never learn how to feel. Then find out that your brother that's ten, is walking around with rocks in his pockets peddling them to lost souls in the concrete jungle. Now my twelve years old sister is having a baby, in love with the molester, sex and crazy.

THOMAS AND SHIRLEY MARSHALL

A love affair born in the Milky Way, two hearts sewn together by the hands of time beating as one. A faithful journey, headed for eternity with all the blessings from the creator. Tee a Libra that has a smile that could charm the sun and can be weighted in the balances, to see which one is warmer. Marcus the Capricorn with eyes brighter, than the stars twinkling in the galaxy with a humble spirit that the angels, sure appreciate. Two grandsons blooming from the family tree, Mekhi who is faster than the wind and the sound of his Virgo laughter has no end. Marcus Jr. stunning to the sight he appeared in our sky on a Leo morning, bring joy with him that will last for eternity.

MY LOVER

Her intellects born in the Milky Way, eyes look like stars twinkling in the night, hands softer than clouds that decorate the sky. Lips sweeter than nectar to a bee, voice always have loving words for me. Hair silky black toss by the wind, roots reaching back to the pyramids. Smile brighter than the moonlight, heartbeats louder than thunder, enough curves to make your mind wonder. Time holds all the keys, love fills each breath she takes, golden tone skin leads her way. Two bloodstreams, knowing that there is no end, dreams do come true. You just have to wait on the one, that's just for you

HEROIN

A thief of souls, black tar gold your best friend are a syringe and spoon, fill with the tears out of broken eyes. Arms littered with track marks, veins will never grow old, because of the pollution they have swallowed. The shadows, that have been cast over hopeless minds for decades continue to blossom. A thirst for serenity is what their spirits lone for, black tar heroin promises to open that window. So that the doomed can see their brilliant, rose colored fantasy land where dreams expire.

I AM SORRY GOD

You gave me this beautiful temple and I defiled it with pollutants on this continent. Temptations no longer grow on trees, there is something called the internet that has brought your servants to their knees. If there ever was a time that humanity needs someone to walk on water. It would be now, before souls be forfeited, the eyes are the offenders and desire is the accomplice. There is nothing left to the imagination, sin has made sure of that, fornicating walks the wind looking for playmates. Chemical addictions decorate the atmosphere, soon there will be nothing dear. Homicides continue to bloom and his twin brother, suicide is growing, love put in its final notice.

THE SUNDOWN TOWNS

Bloodlines are still breathing, dreams stop there, remember there is two water fountains. Both flavors are crayon colors, a line is drawn through the atmosphere. Vanish before your shadow goes to sleep, never forget y'all aren't welcome here. None of the residents take the time to think, that your ancestors were stolen from another continent, that's why yall are suffering in the western hemisphere. Conceived a slave and born a have not to a fate of servitude, there is never any good news. Don't forget that this republic isn't planted for you, so you will never have a view. There have been prophets, that speaks on our behalf, but they were extinguished and laid to rest underneath the grass.

So dry your hearts and lift the voices above the stars and maybe the creator will hear us and take us apart.

MAHANDAS GANDHI

A light wrapped in a loincloth, whose spirit can never be extinguished. His thirst for righteousness began in South Africa, were he went to practice law and felt the racism against the Indian minority. From the mighty British Empire's rigid racial code, that had displaced the natives. Gandhi ignored his lucrative law practice, to lead successful non violent protests that dismantled anti- Indian law in South Africa that awakens later. The wind carried him back to India, where the British Empire also had fingerprints controlling the government. Strangling the natives with rising taxes, and imperialism, that cripples the continent for eternity. Gandhi stand against the British, lead to him being imprisoned for over a decade and eventually to his demise, what a lost to humanity.

NELSON MANDELA

Born free in South Africa in 1918 to a royal family of the Thembu tribe of the Xhosa people. Only to blossom, realizing that apartheid was flourishing him and outspoken leaders were disappearing. Diamonds mines can never hear, the teardrops falling from watery eyes for centuries or see the weeping mothers of the massacred at Sharpeville by the military. Mandela founded the guerrilla wing of the African Nationalist, committing acts of sabotage against the South African apartheid government that had been using war, violence, oppression and impoverishment an entire people. This is what lead to his captivity on Robben Island for more than two decades, where he was tortured and treated inhumanely. Even though he became president, the conditions of the native people continue to deteriorate, insuring that they have no future, and that is still true.

INDIAN SMILE

We have watched the sun bloom each morning for centuries, in North America and witness the closing of its warm eye in the west. Our tepees once shined on the landscape, like stars twinkling in the night. As we sit around the campfires passing the peace pipe. While listening to the wolves singing to the moonlight, what a beautiful sound. Belonging to the earth and be free like the wind, rivers running through our veins that have no ends. Riding horses, watching the eagles patrolling the sky, bison in the fields grazing by, that's a lovely sight.

WHO

Who painted the sky ocean blue and draped it with cirrus clouds to shade you. Who wakes the sun in the east, that warms your heart until it closes its eye in the west. Who gave the wind its breath that shows North, South, East, and West on its way to rest. Who sprinkled the stars across the night sky that twinkles in your eyes so bright. Who hanged the moon that never comes out too soon and if you listen real close it will even tell you when to move. Who planted the flowers, so many different flavors with healing powers. Who can tell me where the adobe of love is, it has help decorate the globe with many beautiful souls. Who knew that rain would nourish the earth and quench our thirst.

I LOVE HIM

He makes my heart run a hundred miles an hour, just by the way his black pupils touch my body. The sound of that encouraging voice, has lifted my spirit, to the third heaven where the divine dwell. those wondering hands knows just what my mind needs, on this journey into ecstasy. Dreams do come true, I know because, I am living in one each morning that, my eyes open, like the sunrise, I am beside my soul mate. The wind will get to whisper about how much that, I love him across the Milky Way. While the moon watches our love blooming for eternity and a shooting stars, gives someone else the desire of their hearts.

CAN I CRY TODAY

The nimbus clouds are gathering around my eyes; the wind began to blow deep down in my mind. The water out of my eyes is drowning my feet, the floodgates burst last week. It has been eight moons since my feelings touched your soul, on this journey searching for love. Your meek nature drew my heart near letting it know that there is nothing to fear. Not knowing that healthcare could hear your anguish during the years. My ears were introduced to the agony that visits you during the night. Not knowing that, I couldn't win this fight. Your voice reaches to the heavens looking for a why, for this curse in your life. It hurts my soul to know that there is no cure for you.

MY GRANDFATHER

Salt and pepper hair, twelve gauge shotgun leaning behind the rocking chair. You could tell the seasons by looking into his eyes, rabbit hunting always makes his heart smile. Tan skin, voice stronger than the wind, sitting by the creek reminiscing about sin. Squirrels jumping from limb to limb, snake climbing up the bank, the sound of the shotgun interrupts the day.

Fishing rods sleeping along the lake, waiting on a feeling that's never too late. Saying that there will be mistakes along the way let your eyes rain and look for another way. Time is a taker, so cherish everyday following a spiritual path, knowing that you won't lose your place.

THE GHOST DANCE

Yellow bird was the choreographer and wounded knee the last dance floor, with snow and bones falling out of the sky. Bullets ring out, spirits expire from the hot shots while conquers watch.

Sitting Bull Prophecy came true, the ghost shirts couldn't protect me or you from a thorn coming through. Drinking from the lakes of old, seeing reflections, I wish that, I could know. Stars have all the knowledge they were here before tomorrow. Riding pass the moon and kissing the earth, earth you finally realize who to trust. Seasons leave so many fingerprints in the sky, seeking a land beyond the milky way were eyes haven't cried.

THE UNDERGROUND RAILROAD

You can't see the tracks with your mind's eye closed, there's no chariots just thirsty souls wearing swaddling clothes. There's no need for a ticket look for the North Star smiling above, it was there before your ancestors were brought ashore. Generations born in bondage, shaped in fear and forced to drink from the cups of misery. Barefoot and cold walking paths of shadows of demise. Hibernating in caves and weeping in cellars at the beginning of light. Parent can't let their children go out to play, because their souls might fly away. Still following the stars by night, hoping that they are leading us right because all that we have to smile about is the moonlight. Tired of drinking the water that flows out of our eyes and tasting the sting of the whip, while walking the cotton field strips. Trying to swim the Ohio River, searching for a candle peeping out of the window, fleeing the slave catchers in the wilderness.

EARTH

I will miss you soon along with all your wounds and wanting souls that will never be hold. My eyes will never see your lovely sun smiling or the wind giving the trees a massage while the birds sing love songs. Volcanoes will continue to erupt because of all the mistrust underneath the crust Earthquakes shakes the turf, shooting stars flee the night our soil is telling us to change. Pollution lives with the wind, nuclear waste hibernates in mountains where there is no end, rivers are fill with water that can't be swallowed. Tears fall from the beautiful blue-sky heart, because of all its lost, while the moon sits by watching.

MARRISA MY NIECE

An angel blossoming in the garden of Eden with eyes brighter than a meteorite. Running from the night and a smile that's warm like the sun that rises in our sight. I am blessed that you are my niece and to see you receive your college degree we are proud of thee. Your grandmother cherishes the day that you came into her life to stay. Bring joy, that can be replaced arid a grandfather. A man of very few words you have feel his heart with so much love. Marrisa on your journey in life, I am sure that God has more duties and blessings waiting on you. So stay faithful and may all the dreams that visit you come true.

TO MY LOVING MOTHER

Mother thank you for the gift of life bring me into your precious life, holding me close and just right before, I was ready to take flight. Your charming voice is always near letting me know that there is nothing to fear guiding my first steps for years. I always knew that your angel arms were near if, I was to ever stumble and fall in this beautiful milky way we call home. Mother you have given me something that, I can never repay you for, I wish that, I could sell the sun to purchase you, a healthier life.

MY MOTHERS DAY

It's not just a single day for Queen that gave breath to my twin brother, and I in a time of trials. We were poor but your love never let us know, why we were going in the back door. When illness found our days your angel arms stayed up all night holding us tight making sure that we were alright. But one of us wouldn't see another sunlight, a soul went back to the creator never being able to fly. Always keeping your Queen spirit faithful, my love for you is eternal, roses do grow in racism just look at us. You leading the way to ideology with a soul commitment, to praying for a brighter existence on a continent of dreamers.

REGRET

Knows the address to my soul, the paternity question always takes a hold. Sin took control of my life, at fifteen years old, leading me into a pair of deceitful arms. That handicapped my future, on this odyssey through the milky way, where eyes keep secrets and hearts tell lies. But the moon knows that, I have doubts, he heard me reminiscing a deity. About fingerprints, that are getting ready to bloom in the garden of life. It causes my mind to have discomfort to know that, unfaithfulness has played a part in my existences.

XAVIER

The sun shining in my life if only, I was there to hold you tight instead of following the stars into the night. Abandoning my seed to grow alone in this garden of trials and tribulation. You are the most wonderful seed a father can have so always be strong and proud. It's not your fault for what fate has done, I am the one that drifted away from your sky. What a tragedy that has came to be because my life has never been complete, wearing around this emptiness.

I will always have a void in my soul for you and though I have never been there for you does not mean that, I don't cherish you. Late at night while laying in the dark, I often look out my window at the moon and wonder how you are now that, I am so far off

FORGIVENESS

The spirit asks for it, to help ease the years, the wind doesn't know, where it lives and snow can't cover it up. Water won't drown it, fire can't burn it, eyes have never seen it, time carries it. Ice won't freeze it, forgiveness can't be buried because dirt is afraid of it. Death has hide from it, hearts seek after it, hands can't touch it feet has trespassed against it, and gold can't buy it. The sun doesn't know its zip code, a shooting star once tried to find it. Tears wonder about it, only the soul holds the key to forgiveness.

VALENTINE'S DAY

A day that could never express how much that, I adore you because every day you are my heart's desire. My spirit loves to hear your sweet voice while laying there in the dark in each others' arms whispering words of passion. That echoes deep down in my soul when, I think of the love that we share together in this galaxy of wonders were hearts run free.

MRS JEAN MCCLOUD

A loving Queen, Mother and Grandmother, the earth is
blessed because of you. Your eyes have touched the east and
west coast on your journey in life. The caring smile that you
carry helps spirit along the way and the kind words spoken
brightens their days. The oil paintings that you create will
bring joy to heartbeats for generations to come. The smooth
detail strokes of the paintbrush on the canvas will keep pupils
captivated into the next earth age.

THE LOVE OF MY LIFE

You said that you have dexorocardia sipus inversus, born ninety three degrees west longitude, and thirty-three degrees north latitude. On a Libra morning underneath a Magnolia sky with silky black hair playing in the light. Brown irises that have no end with a voice stronger than a typhoon. Speaking lyrics that can help humanity began again, lead by her banana painted skin. The contents of her soul rules my domain, when my spirit was wondering alone. Her love reached out to me letting me know that, I will always have a home.

Yes storms may come, but remember that we hibernate in the Milky Way, there will be space debris.

THE BIBLE

Is a map that leads to treasure that's far beyond this Universe, there are ten truths that must be followed along the way. You don't need transportation charity and faith will carry us along the journey. Away from the valley of the shadows of death, were storms come often and lives search for eternity. There is a light that shines brighter the sun and will warm deep down in our souls. Once we open our spiritual eyes and tune our ears to humanity heartbeats. Then we will know how to cross the river of compassion and know the true meaning of the bible.

I WILL SEE YOU IN HEAVEN

The soul knows the way, but the flesh keep trying to lead it astray. Because the carnal mind has so much to say, after witnessing what the eyes have tasted. ON this odyssey through the solar system, were greed comes often and unfaithfulness runs free. The heart's thirst can never be satisfied, while wanting fingerprints can't be numbered. Find the path, that the vultures eyes have never seen and death doesn't know how to locate it. Nirvana can hear, our spirits crying out in the wilderness, wanting rest from a dictatorship.

I MISS LOVING YOU

Another dream of you visited me last night, only to vanish into the morning sunlight. The sound of your celestial voice echo, deep down in my soul, when the wind shows. It seems like yesterday that my heartbeats, follow your starry eyes across the universe. To paradise were love grows real, and iniquity has no dominion. It has been half a decade, since your breath expired, leaving me with all the whys. The moon knows truths that the finite mind is not able to comprehend, about deaths beginning.

MY MOTHER'S BIRTHDAY

Is so special because if not for it, I wouldn't exist. The love that she has shown me continues to water my soul and her faithfulness to spirituality is something to behold. A living example of a saint sowing words of wisdom that will help humanity blossom. May your light continue to shine for all eternity like a star in the night. So that wandering spirits can find their place in this ocean of life.

ESSIE MAE WHITLOCK
Aunt Doot

A beautiful soul growing in the garden of Eden you have brought so much beauty into the garden. All that one must do is to look at, the flowers that have bloomed from you, a loving mother with a heart of gold. That lives in a brick house that sits off a country dirt road. I enjoy visiting Aunt Doots, besides her sweet voice and caring smile, it's like going to the zoo there are animal, that decorate the property that we can't wait to see. There is even a creek running through too, with a vegetable garden planted in view. Holidays are special just because of you, I get to feel your warm hugs and taste your sweet blackberry and apple pies. You have truly been a blessing in my life and I love you.

THE DARK CONTINENT

Twenty degrees east longitude thirty degrees north latitude. There is D.N.A. born here that's more valuable than diamonds and gold. If not for it North America wouldn't have grown, eyes waking up on a Red, White, and Blue republic. Palms that will never remember touching the pyramids and lips that won't drink from the Nile, Heartbeats that talk to the stars, wanting to know where to start, trying to run away from history that inhumane. Eyes continue to migrate to Africa from other continent because petroleum quenches their thirst and the environment is left to suffer. Tyrants rule the countries with platoons of wrenched spirits, that have homicide in their hearts, saying that ideology plays a role. A single virus owns acres across the continent, and slavers fingerprints were first discovered here.

THE POOR

Will our eyes always drop water, like the spring rain falling from heaven, while stomach cry out in hunger. The shacks that hold our destitute shadows, has seen too much pain in this land of classes. Dreams come often, invading hopes with mirages. when eyelids open, leaving the spirit hopeless. The dust calls out our names, will stumbling blocks ever change, the poor is older than hurt. I wish that, I could sell the stars, to buy us a new birth right. We all have the same sun that warms our bones, and water quenches our flesh. But the moon is the only one, that the have nots can trust.

LITTLE HOMELESS BOY

Trying to return to a cocoon that time has already consumed he has slumbered and whelped underneath bridges, and in cardboard boxes. Panhandling and eating out of garbage cans, to quench his thirsty frame, that has felt too much blame. Alone still trying to find the meaning for all the storms, while following the stars by site. Hoping they can lead him to a society, that's not frightening and careless before his demise.

Looking at life through his poverty eyes has destroyed the only heart. That he will ever feel, living on the street.

CANDLE IN A CAGE

To be held so long that time has left you, fate walked away, and you are outside of grace. The projects that worked on you so long disappeared to go on their own. After a while, in the corridors in their mind they decide to go up to the cage to release the candle, on their way, they realize that the candle has been in the cage so long where would it go. Since you don't need the shadows anymore, the wind started to show, knocking on the door. Wanting to know, if the candle needs a ride away from your shore, holding its breath making sure not to blow.

MORRIS-VILLAGE

Sits alone with many thirsty souls resting in her arms. Their eyes reaching beyond the stars, hearts beating all alone. Voices looking for another time zone, ears tired of going on underneath this morning sun, carrying burdens from around the globe. Wandering through time trying to find something to hold, tears falling from deep down inside this void. That's filled with all this poison, that blooming in all nations torn apart.

Morris-Village admires beggars, and icons they will for eternity have a place in her heart. Psychologist taking walks into festering souls, that have never been known from times of cold. Minds born into harm's way, waiting on them to come out and play, with addictions that are here to stay.

ON THE ROAD TO FREEDOM

We've been traveling since the beginning of dawn on this slippery surface and yielded to the worse that time has to offer. The cross roads have separated us as a family in this valley of self. Eyes are our only road blocks, can a deity help. There has been enough blood flowing in the streams of minds. That has over flooded the hearts on the road to freedom. Mortals need to find their way, to the table of humanity. Because all that we have is one sun, that cries for us, and a moon that is embarrassed. Along with a sky, that is ashamed of what it sees breathing underneath it.

STATUE OF LIBERTY

You were born in France and traveled across the Atlantic ocean to stand tall in a harbor for humanity to see for a race that couldn't speak. A crown on your head to show that you are truly a Nubian queen with a manuscript in your left hand litter with fables. A scepter with a diamond in your right hand held up to the sky for all to see passing in the future. Looking for freedom, be careful don't let your mind deceive you a heart has many faces it can never please you. Dressed in a beautiful evening gown that hangs down to your feet shackles and chains peeping from underneath. Hoping that justice can't see them, helping hold souls captive for centuries.

TO MY MOTHER

So Dear and special to me, rising me up in this world to see all the beautiful things, I am to be. Guiding my steps when, I couldn't see. Staying up late at night with me when, I was ill and couldn't slumber. I have prayed to God thanking him for my mother's touch. Alone she learned this cruel system and became strong carrying us along the way. Teaching us about a home that's not made from wood, stones and the foundation isn't the earth. Still following the stars by night hoping that they are leading, your heart right. Casting your net into the sea you gave me something to believe in. That eyes can't see, and hands can't touch it, it's a spiritual must.

A'NAYAH

My precious diamond blooming within me, a gift from the creator that, I am anxious to see. I often feel thee, moving so secretly before dawn, awaking me in this beautiful garden of life. Where there are shooting stars for you to wish upon and dreams do come true, just take a look at you. A'nayah the sun rises to warm your charming soul and give light to your steps, so always watch out for stumbling blocks. Rainy days are necessary to quench the earth's thirst, so always take care of her. Snow will come visit, but may not stay long, so hold on to memories and keep them warm. Birds sing to you know that, they are there for you so always be true. Remember that there is no gulf that will ever keep me away from you. Flowers grow to show you that there is a beauty that's not formed by mans hands, so that you know that there is no end.

If you listen close, when the wind shows you will hear it say mommie loves you.

LOOK AT WHAT'S GOING ON IN OUR WORLD

Let's take a walk beyond the stars and look at, what's being developed before we all dissolve. The sun is ashamed of what it sees and water quenches our hunger. The wind often shows up and we don't know where it's visiting us from or where its traveling to. The rain has been falling from humanity's soul for hundreds of years ,but mortals still can't feel. War pollutes the land while the moon sits and stares. Respect lost its way, pestilence has millions of friends, bitterness has no ends. There won't always be a currency to put you in a class, poverty flows through time holding minds. The plantations of concrete and steel litter the landscapes of the western hemisphere and research comes before babies being born in hopelessness.

SOMETIMES DREAMS DON'T COME TRUE

I survive in a concrete jungle, and a capitalistic sky is all that, I see predators and outlaws roam the streets. Death row is where my mama breathes, she murdered a trick during a robbery. That's what my grandmother told me she is the family tree. So many branches have fallen asleep from a epidemic, I wonder if heaven got a concrete jungle in it. Angels turned into zombies by addictions, polluting the streams that run through veins riding a needle flowing on a spoon. To ·see lost souls suffering, underneath a broken Red sun, White lies, and a Blue republic. Sometimes it makes me ask the creator why.

LOST

I lost my continent, family tree, name, language, religion, and freedom to kidnappers with their colleagues' murderers. Only to be trapped in servitude, in the Milky Way, were death comes often and drugs run free.

My great grandfather and mother were born slaves, my grandfather was a homicide victim, found beside a cold South Carolina dirt road. I never knew my grandmother, they said that the north star lead her away from a lot of abuse and hatred. My father was lost to moonshine and illiteracy, the republic didn't want him to see the real reason for his misery. While a disability took my mother's love, leaving me without ever knowing that feeling.

Adultery found my eyes sight as, I walked across the stars, now all that I am left with is a broken heart. A syringe assisted my younger brother with his demise, now the sun doesn't have to continue watching him expire on the inside. S.I.D.S, came by after only, one hundred and eighty days, escorting infant daughter back to paradise, were there is only light.

END TIMES

Armageddon is being held in the garden of Eden mortals from winds are gathering there. Like eagles preying on a spring day, where the Tigris and Euphrates rivers meet. The sky is filled with flying locust of steel, spitting lightning bolts at will. I often wonder what kind of humanity, I am breathing in. Mothers are being extinguished with their seeds still hibernating in the cocoon, adolescents are missing all around the globe. Gardens of stones paint the landscapes of time at moments, I wish that I were deaf and blind. The prophet's visions are living, famine and pestilence are thriving a large part of mankind is vanishing. Look to the northern heavens for a reason, while the stars are fleeing.

GRANDMAMAS BURDEN

Young seed growing up in the wild life, you better slow down these roads are rough. Floating around on four with your pants hanging low inhaling smoke from a plant you didn't grow. Eyes closed all day and creeping out late at night with plants in plastic bags. Peddling them to the lost souls that don't know which way to flow.

Grandmama's burden has never had a mom or dad in sight, they took the nearest flight. She has done everything in her might to make his world bright, before her light burns out. Will he always travel around with a slow form of suicide, with felonies in his mind. No respect of any kind, living blind he doesn't know that he is running out of time.

FORGOTTEN FRUIT

For fathers kidnapped and enslaved, our grandparents birth in captivity their seeds planted in misery and blooming in poverty. Still flowing the stars by night, but there's not a safe galaxy in sight. After sailing hundreds of years with thousands of hearts fill with tears. Pain and suffering have them praying to a deity, to let them expire because they can't face the plight. Justice standing over there with a blindfold on covering lying eyes. Pretending that she can't see, the strange fruit hanging from the oak trees for centuries.

REFUGEES

We only had a twinkling of an eye to grab, our offspring step over the extinguished that decorate the landscape and flee in the wilderness. Our broken souls litter the highways of humanity, the tears from our hearts have made the volcano ash so hard that, there is nowhere for us to plant the expired. Nothing blooms from the earth here and the wind never had time to learn our names. All of our stars fell in Africa, have we all forgotten that we are from the tribes of the dust.

Baptized in the Nile and weaned from yesterday, fingerprints running from the minds of time.

YESTERDAY

Everyday someone says forget about yesterday and, I say maybe you can show me the way. Because all the roads that, I have followed brings me back the same way. Is there possibly a map or stars that leads the way from yesterday. Are maybe, give back the regret that grew along the days and find the voice that, I betrayed.

That, I wish was here to hold me tight and say, I love you by the way.

WASTED TIME

We have sun that warms our organs, stars that lead us astray and a moon that's never shy. Getting down on my knees praying to a God that, they say can't be seen with the pupils.

While trying to pick up the pieces of my damaged mind.

My spirit is broken from trying to live in another mortal's dreams. In pursuit of helping to quench their thirst, before we return to the dust. Looking back at my life in the rearview mirror of time, I finally realize that the flesh won't be satisfied, and time can't be harnessed.

UNCLE ODELL WILLIAMS

A mentor that help guide me through life, when there wasn't a star for me to follow. Leading by example a career lawman that would give his existence to protect society. Traveling across states lines, riding the wind hunting desperados until the end. A father, husband, brother and friend a loving spirit that came to an end. What a tragedy, the world has lost one of its brightest stars.

THE SUN

The keeper of the earth, a passenger in the sky, warmer than the human body and we don't know why. Sometimes you are cold and at times you take a six month vacation depending on where we hibernate. You have been· here since the dawn of time, I often wonder who could have been your mother.

Because she was so kind to leave you behind to make friends with the moon and the wind. Sitting like a diamond in a ring watching, when love had its first dream. On the pillow of humanity along the Nile River, warming the souls of the pyramid thinkers. While waiting on the ideology takers, to paint the landscapes of minds on the roads of time.

KIMBERLY

Laying here watching the sun peeping out of the east, thinking about the life that I throw away and the one that I chose, and it hurts, like a star leaving the moon. If only there was a seer that, I could have went to before that, Independence Day was born maybe, I wouldn't be so torn. At the moment, I thought that, I was sad now, I know what sadness really is, Kimberly laying here thinking of you and your love, I once knew. It seems like yesterday that, I ate from a forbidden life, being deceitful to thee. The cold winds have begun to show again, and my heart can't take them anymore.

Feeling the trauma from the life that, I chose and the anguish that lingers through my soul.

NEW LOVE

Her smile is warmer than the sun, eyes bright as the stars guiding in the night, with hair soft like a cloud. Ears are attentive to my spirits needs, knowing that it has been neglected, for three hundred years. Voice speaking words that my soul, has been yearning to hear, her mind comprehends how, I feel. Two heart beating together in the garden of eternity, and minds blossoming beside the river of time. Arms holding each other, during the endless moonlight, palms never thought twice. Feet running past the wind, to tell humanity, about a love that has no sin.

SEEING LOVE

Her face is more beautiful than the sky and the sparkling of her eyes is what my love follows. Her sweet lips whisper words that my heart yearns to feel and her skin shines, like gold in the sunlight. Diamonds said that she was more precious than them. To see, the way that the wind tosses her hair, always draws me near. Stars come out at night just to see her and the moon ask her for advice. On this voyage into paradise where time stands still, and love roams at will. Roses bloom just to be a gift to her and pearls swim ashore, knowing that they can be a part of her life. Birds think that it's an honor to rehearse for her, while holidays thank her for being around. The seasons enjoy coming, because of her, even water loves touching her. Air said that it was a pleasure to serve her and being a Goddess clarifies her breath.

DEAR SISTER

A life of discontent has come my way, dimming the sunlight that warms the days. A lot of my dreams left yesterday abandoning me alone in this desolate place. My heart drips blood when I think of the trespasses that I against you in my world of addiction. Where, I am not proud of what, I have become along the road of life. I apologize to you for all the pain that, I cause your heart and ask God for a new start. Dear Sister thanks to God, you have been an inspiration in our lives. Since mother was laid to rest, after giving us her best. You have two beautiful flowers of your on, blooming in your angel arms, fill with love.

Yet, you still have the mother's touch, for your younger siblings, and you are sure appreciated.

WHY I DRINK

To help wash away the dust out of my mind, freeing me from this place in time, swallowing a childhood that was so unkind. Searching for some kind of peace, deep down in my soul, gulping a half a quart a day traveling on my way Old time, why have you been so blind, showing grief in my stars, leading me to a place fill with sorrow. All that magic portions have done, is make things more difficult for me, as if, I couldn't see. Something's in life, you will never get over, you just have to put them in the ocean.

MT. EVEREST

So tall and proud you have been breathing for millions of moons, even the clouds bow down to you. You don't need air or water to continue to exist, your temperature is coldest on earth, snow and ice is your coat. Mortals love trying to creep up and down your body, knowing that they may even expire. Dreaming of touching the top of your head before they retire, all one must do is to look at all the oxygen bottles that litter your body. Then see the deceased, that have never left you, that have no tombstones with a clue, they too have became a part of you. Leaving love ones with nothing to view.

DIVINE

Her eyes are stars twinkling in my life, with silky black hair that matches the night. The sweetness of her lips has my spirit conquered, as the wind carries the sound of her sound of her adorable voice into my soul. The charming smile that's on her face warms my world in this Milky Way, we call home. The moonlight gets to watch our love affair bloom into, one of the seven wonders of the globe. Fate has truly been a blessing to me, by allowing my breath to grow eternally with another spiritual being.

WE WILL MEET AGAIN

Where eyes don't judge you by, what type of skin clothes you have on, or the sound of your voice, only your inner contents. Hearts loving the entire rainbow, not the flavor that broken tongues speaks, on their journey of misery. Minds awaking in another galaxy, were hands don't practice breaking the commandments, atomic energy has never been conceived, and spirits aren't contaminated. In a time, that has no pestilence coming ashore, and pollution never found the way. Children can go out and play, mothers don't have to worry, about them disappearing, and souls have control of their rights, death has no site.

THUG LIFE

Born to a thirteen year old in poverty, a cloud of conspiracy visits were street pharmacists rule the concrete jungle. Mama bless her soul, we never had anything, we were homeless when she was fifteen. Along the road of hopelessness, she lost her dreams at sixteen. That's when, crack cocaine found its way into her stream, to quench her thirst, she started laying with the worst, and that's how she caught the curse. Leaving her seed, blowing in the concrete jungles wind, his pants, hanging below his waist, and he has a flag tied around his head. He didn't go to school to learn sign language, but it hangs around him. Scars and tattoos tell the allegories of his trials, and tribulations, the homies Showed him, where the rocks play at, so late at night, he finds his way there. Where addictions live, and the only ones that care and gunshots often ring out from hopeless minds. Before, any tongue judge me, take a peep, at what society dealt me, a life of emptiness, and misery all that, I see for the future is federal confinement. Late at night in my dreams, I am counting tombstones, everyone that, I love has expired.

SOUTH CAROLINA ON MY MIND

I've pack my saddlebags and dried my eyelashes. My iron horse is waiting outside, I am on my way to where the suns born. It has been sixty moons since, I road west, on trail forty into the arms of regret. Still following the stars by sight, finally realizing that my breath don't fit into where, my desire lay. South Carolina on my mind, passing by memories from times of joy, seeing a spirit, that once held my heart.

Aristotle, said that Osiris can't change the pass, sure wish that wasn't true, because the only love that, I would ever feel, lives there. Decades have vanished like a vapor, elements that had value are meaningless, and all that, I have to show for my existence is a desecrated soul.

SADE

You are the sun that rises in my soul, and the stars twinkling in my spirit, your love makes my heart dream. When, I was lost the winds of time guided you into my life. The charming smile that you carry gives me light, every since the first time my eyes touch you. My life hasn't been the same, the love that I have for you will never change. When, I think of you it brings joy into my world, giving me a son along with your love. Walking through life, cherishing each day and night, with the loves of my life, that's what makes breathing so nice.

MY EX WIFE

It's been over a decade, since my infidelity lead you away, I sure wish that it was some kind of a way for you to have forgiven my trespasses against you. The creator doesn't have a more loving soul, blooming in his garden of life.

Every since you drifted away out of my sky, breathing hasn't been so bright. My mind miss knowing that you loved me in this endless sea. Where storms come often wondering flows free, have I lost the only love that my nature will ever see, my heart is still holding on to memories. Hearing your voice, speaking in the wind, passing by spirits from times of old, reminiscing about palms, I miss loving.

ANNIE L STEED
Great Grandmother

Thanksgiving and Christmas has pass like the smell of your pies, that once filled the adobe. I sure miss, seeing the caring smile that covers your face with grace, and the sound of your voice echoing in my heart. From the encouraging words that continue to be a guiding light in in my life, and you have been right. I often think about, when we use to sit on the front porch, you in your rocking chair. Dipping your redman snuff, reminiscing about your adolescent life on the reservation of mistrust. Were you use to pick cotton, from dawn to dust pulling a cotton sack up and down rows from times of old, and the sun showing no love. Sweat burning eyes, fingertips raw, backs hurting, souls can't take anymore, and minds have lost hope.

A WASTED LIFE

The western hemisphere is where, I weep, the Atlantic ocean escorted my D.N.A here. My dreams never bloom, in this, soil, fifty stars are standing guard. While seven red, unclean spirits take charge, defiling the minds with chemical dependency, along with his colleague depression. While the bodies are deteriorating from viruses, that scientist reminisce about. Ideology leaders are lecturing, but the followers continue to wither, in a hopeless soil. Racism will always bloom, it has the electoral votes from forty colonies, and congress. The poor can't be numbered, and a crooked heart, will never be straight, but one thing is for sure, death is waiting.

WANDERING SOULS

Will you ever be hold, seeking around these shores, casting shadows on floors, knocking on doors hoping to be heard. Painting the landscape with verbs, reaching back in time trying to find courage to solve the riddle of life. Looking for the wind, to carry thee away from things that are soon to be. But you still can't see, the Nile River that carried, we form the lower valley to the sea. Wandering souls captured behind so many doors, wondering their plains, trying to find a reason, to lead thee away from things that will never be.

Traveling thousands of years to see, the waterfalls to be, carving grooves in hearts passing we. Drinking from the cup of life, that harnessed the broken as it may be. Place your heart in a balance beside a feather and you may live forever.

SEEING REGRET

My eyes are raining this morning, in the land of the fallen, dreams often visit me, that holds me hostage. My heart awakes beside regret, I often wonder about, who gave me feelings, I sure wish, they had thought twice. The path that I chose lead me to this place in my life, where, I hibernate. I never thought that regret, would have a name face, legs and a voice. When, I go to my deity in prayer, I often wonder if, I am heard. When we eminence, about if regret will bloom in my soul until, I am cold. Touching regret for the last decade, has turn my spirit poor, knowing that, I am the one, who created this sea of foes.

THE SPHINX

Born of limestone, and wean from the Nile, your majestic headdress brings out those endless eyes. That seen monotheism conceives, in an Egyptian heart, and spread across minds without the sea being parted. Sitting there in a pose, that time won't forget, it was there, when your birthday took its first breath. Protector of the pyramids that sparkle, like stars in the sky. The wind comes often to visit, whispering Pharaohs fame, that decorate the plains and museums around the globe.

REMEMBERED

To be remembered above a whisper, wondering if you could hear me from here because, I sure miss you. Wishing that we could have been born in a cleaner stream, never taking away from how much we mean. A flash of light, then an image, on a piece of paper appears, will you please wait for me. The days are slowly disappearing, and the nights come visit so often, I have begun to miss them. The swim that we took, bring me back to the nets that captured us, like all the jewels of the sea, were we just end up in someone's jewelry box to see. Life is made up of memories wash me off and you will see.

LOVE **CHANGES**

You fly away in a bird of steel, to new palms, staying away five nights not caring how, I feel laying here each second with my eyes fill with tsunami. Looking out of my bedroom window at the moon, and stars wondering if they can hear my heart thundering. The water that flows down my cheeks is warm, but takes no form, it just changes with the four season abandoning me without reason. Love changes that's what unfaithfulness puts you through, turning the soul into an iceberg. Causing the spirit to have a relationship with a deity to help calm the gales, living deep inside, that's what love does to you.

ROSELYN

I often reminisce, about the day that my spirit first touch you, while traveling down the hall of wisdom. Beautiful frame, thirsty brown eyes carrying a charming smile, with honey colored skin following you ·around. Long silky black hair dancing in the wind, a voice whispering words that have no end. You took my soul, and lead it away, letting me know that, a rose would be blooming from you at a later place. Nine moons later, no gate could block the day, a little princess came out to stay, leaving loving memories across my heart, that can never be erased. As you continue to blossom on your journey down the road of life, keep smiling like the sun, and always think thrice.

MARTHA PAGE

A light that has been shining in God's garden of life so long having a heart warmer than the sun. A loving mother, and wife that guides her family, like the stars in the night, you have truly been a gift to our lives. A mighty woman of God, whose faith can never be scared and as sure as there is a heaven, laying beyond the universe there is a place for you in God's heart. Martha Page your love has covered many lives like the sand along the sea shore, and your spiritual voice has encouraged us. You are an inspiration to many souls and we will always love you.

DEAR GRANDSON MALCOLM

Open your eyes, and read the signs, as you walk down the road of time, and remember the choices you make can turn you blind. In a society, where things aren't always what they seem to be, unfaithfulness often comes out to stay. Be strong and always look to the sky and give a master's degree everything that you got. You are going to need it, to help you fly in this democratic empire, were many spirits are on the decline.

My grandson always be a leader, and not a follower, looking to build your own tomorrow.

JEALOUS

Jealous of the wind it has no end, it's been blowing through minds for millenniums and of water, because everyone loves it. While stars are floating by, heading for the soul, it knows the mean of life. Jealous of the sun, it has all of the fun, living ninety three million miles away. Eyes all around the globe love seeing your smiling face and feeling the warmth of your touch. Jealous of the moon it has sewn together hearts across time, decorating the Milky Way with flavors of the human family, and of the dust, because it accepts all of us.

THE OLD MAN

The old man must be evicted, from inside of me, he has taken me down theses paths of darkness, into the dens of sin. As I take inventory of my life, I am ashamed of what, I see, what's even more appalling is that, I have been breathing this way for a quarter a century. I must finally ask myself do, I adore me, because inhaling a slow form of suicide, into my body and hibernating in a cell is not showing love to yourself. Reaching out but feeling emptiness that, I have created, it's time for me, to search my soul, so that my mind can see. Because looking through my eyes have me shaped in iniquities, it's time to harness my untamed existence.

BURDENS

Hi broken seeds blooming in jungles of concrete and steel, where you have lost your light. Both male and female have became a disgrace, leaving the babies seeds, to waste away in the latter years. No road maps to lead their way, through the valleys of North America were addictions come out to live. Their fathers are incarcerated out of states, waiting on a date, being nourished by a system that has fail them. No mothers to hold them near, what a sad life that will soon appear, where is Moses to lead them out of bondage into another galaxy. They are left to drown in their own tears, surrounded by all these stars, getting down on their knees praying to a deity to please don't let us all fall.

I HURT DAVID

Close your ears, you may not want to see what, I did to a glowing spirit, that the creator gave me. Born on a continent, that will never heal, to ancestors, whose blood was often spilled.

Not having a star, to guide me right, I started to play, with the thing in the night. My breath didn't turn out so bright, ten years old, inhaling smoke from the stems, of the cannabis leafs. While swallowing, the water that's brewed, down by the creek, underneath the moonlight. Living a life, with a heart feel with disappointment, and a medulla oblongata that never seen love, in the solar system of failing souls.

OSIRIS
My Grandson

Little king, conceived in the Milky Way of harm, always keep your eyes on your mother's heart. She has seen many stars fall from this capitalistic sky, on this road of life.

Follow the dreams that visit you in the night, and remember a doctrine degree, will make your life bright. No matter, what shakes the earth, keep your head up high because I am always on your side, riding with you until the end of the wind.

MY MAMA IS HURTING

The sky is cloudy today, seems like it's been that way every since, we showed our face. We have traveled these dark roads too many times before, if only the water out of the Nile River, we could drink, maybe our spirits wouldn't sink. I am finished with the life that, I have been wearing around so long, underneath this republic, where there is too many storms. It hurts me to listen to my mama's voice, telling me that, she adores me while sitting behind a T.V monitor. Mama we have face the hardest times, that can be imagine many moments, I have watch you hold back the raindrops from falling from your tired eyes. While wondering about, why time has dealt us a wanting hand.

409 W. MAIN ST

Stooping down behind a mountain as if. I am not seen, the clouds riding by knowing that, I live downstream. Mothers are at church playing the tambourines, sister Mary speaking in tongue, I wonder if they know what it means. The raindrops have begun to from the smoky gray sky, hope they are clean. Because every since we moved beside this pool hall, I have become unclean if you know what, I mean. Pops in the back yard, working on the old sixty-seven Ford Fairlane, times flying by hope that, I am The funeral home is next door, the business is flourishing, there are a lot of souls knocking on heaven's door.

RENEE SMILE

Too young to a face so stern, eyes wandering around in your head like they aren't yours. Living in a castle, with twenty two doors and twenty five windows with no cracks in the floor. It has enough bricks in it to build a pyramid, and the wood in it could be a forest, you know that your ancestors will help you harvest a tomorrow. There are three chariots, waiting on you to chose, the one you dream of, and a trust fund with your autograph attached to it, and you think you got it bad.

BUTTERFLY

Butterfly blooming in a concrete nightmare, where storms come and felons roam free. She never knew her dad, a registered offender, he ran away with a glass stem. Before she could speak, he loves inhaling smoke from the coca leafs. That has lives, under siege that that will never be devoted to anything but chasing smoke, that has no hope. Her mama was an adolescent that the streets swallowed up, a thirteen year old, with a harlots touch. The civilization that they are exhaling in is declining, hopelessness owns the horizon. Pestilence are rising, stealing the souls of the deprived.

TOO LATE

Born in abhor is there any way to escape, to another time and date. Not wishing to live that fate, trying to wake them up, but is it too late. The fountains that they have been drinking from, are out of date and as soon as possible should be replaced. You wonder why adolescents don't want to take your place, look at the images they face, a child doesn't know how to abhor until brought up to date. The fruit, from the trees that they will be eating from, has grown old and perhaps been left out in the cold.

REFUND

As, I stand in the line at the register of life, the gentleman with the nail prints in his hands asked me could he help me, and I replied yes. I need a refund, for being born underneath this ocean colored sky, only to be prey. Breathing for capitalist consumption, never to inherit a family tree, what a tragedy in this ocean, of the free.

TREE

My six feet-eight inch cellie, that downstairs from me, who's extremities hang out the bunk, but you can't see. He often reminisces to my ears, about things his eyes have seen, but will his soul ever be clean. He spends a lot of his minutes on the plasma screen, sleeves rolled up if you know, I mean forgetting about his dreams. Holding his breath until his cares left, will he ever see that he needs help. Tree the only ball that he will ever score with is an eight ball, and its white with no feelings, it even talks with him, but does he really know what it's saying. It stays up late with him and might even leave him deceased. Along the way he stumbled over a check book and started signing his autograph. Because his thirst can't wait, and now he has
a date with a federal fate.

GRATEFUL

Grateful to the sun, because you have warmed creations hearts, and gave love its first start, while living in the sky with the moon, and stars. Grateful for Africa, the garden of Eden were my ancestors began breathing, and began building the pyramids, along the Nile while the sphinx sits there smiling. Grateful to America, because this is where, I took my first breath, and for the plantation in South Carolina, where my mother and father took their first steps. Grateful to Socrates, my father figure, he taught me how to diagnose a republic, and try to cure it, even if the emperor wants you to or not. Grateful for the dust, because that's, where my flesh is going to rest after this test.

STARTING OVER

The flood waters have subsided, and my mind is on dry thought I will soon release my feeling in search of a soul mate.

Attempting to find, a place where my love will be safe, underneath this democracy sky. I can't continue having this thorn in my heart, I've never had an adobe, as long as, I have been breathing or a concubine to call my own. My soul, feels abandon it has been on so many odysseys, now its tired, it's not fair that, I continue to treat it this way. It needs real love, love that can't be brought, with or without plastic money. I've never felt love in my sight, even as a child, from a king or queen, like you feel, the heat from the sun. My wandering spirit has no more trails to follow, the winds of time, has swept them away, is it, the end of my dreams.

PUT IT ALL

As your shadow wonders on this earth, events are going to happen to you that you can't change. Tears that flow down cheeks can't wash them away, thoughts that linger in you won't dismiss the space. Being not conceived would have helped you stay, but you had nothing to do with who went out to play. Trying to run away, but never getting far there are too many stars blocking my heart. Casting all the trespasses against me, into the wind maybe it can take them to their end.

KEEP YOUR MIND UP

The sun May not be smiling for you, it may have taken a day off look at, what it sees. While the moon spent a night alone, just reach on faith, it has all the truths. Hope carries two keys, never forget your knees, thing you view, help you not to believe. Charity can warm the soul, just try it and receive, giving isn't, always in objects. Spirituality can keep you warm, even if your heart, may not feel love in this realm. Patience, and the wind has all been friends, even the moonlight can't remember your sins The foundation means, it can begin again, two rainbows in the sky, pink, yellow and ocean green.

THE SHOE SHINE MAN

Putting bright smiles on every pair of shoes, that meet his hands, he has visitors from the four winds of the land. A tall slender with one ring on his left hand, and glasses on his smiling face, sparkling shoes leads, his way through the day. The Beau Rivage is where his stand stays, and his clients often come out to play the games there. Win or lose the shoes stop there, to get the shine, put on their face with love and care.

BLANDINA

A vessel of faith, you were tuckered all day in the arena even the lost souls that cheered on, was astonished at your threshold for pain. And the only thing you had to do, to escape, was to denounce your faith, a mother, daughter, and greatest all, a saint. Your frail body took all that it could take, the hot iron chair was your last fate.

Rest now your faithful soul, in the creators' bosom, tell him of all the burdens that are carried by transgressors who can only see in the dark. While in you they can find light and rest, after the labor of this test.

WHERE

Are you at, when my feelings are ignored, where are you, when no one needs to know, and my eyes are overflowing. while my fist, are knocking on the door, and my dreams need, someone to hold. Where you at, when time leaves me alone, and the four winds have gone home. Where are you at, when my voice, needs someone to feel it, and my mind isn't strong enough, to heal it. Where are you at, when no one is home and my love needs to be shown. Where are you at, when my heart needs a break, and the sun isn't warm. While the moon, and stars have moved on, to find a galaxy, where there are no storms. Where are you at, when my future has no form, time has expired, and there is no heaven, for me to Rome.

DR. SHEILA
Evangelist

A messenger from the creator's heart, with the diagnosis, and cure for humanity's transgressions. Her angel voice whispers the words, that will guide your soul, to eternal life. The light, light that she listens to will never be silent, reading eyes like they are parables, reminiscing with them about crosses they are escorting. Letting them know that, the trails won't last forever, and that judgment day will soon be held in heaven. So dry your watery eyes on a nimbus cloud and reach out on faith, because it is the only way. Dr. Sheila a walking example of faith, with silky black hair down to her waist, brown irises leads the way. India smile brightens many days.

I WILL NEVER

See the love smiling in a bride's eyes, while hearing the vows meant for a lifetime, or go on a honeymoon that didn't come to soon. Know the sound of a spouse's voice saying I am and it's a blessing, to live my life with you as a family. No children to carry on my name, there will never be a soul soul mate to claim, a journey down the path of life alone facing the winters of discontent; with a empty heart, while my hair turns to gray, along the way. There will never be a suring, whispering voice laying beside me, in the moonlight lifting up my spirit to new heights. Never to receive a father day card or any holiday gift, with the words simply, I love you. Living a memory less existence, underneath this endless sun, where souls turn cold, and trust may never be known.

MY HEART

Purer than an embryo in a mother's stream soft as the cirrus clouds riding the wind. Warmer than the sun smiling in the sky, bright as a star twinkling in the night. Quieter than a butterfly hovering by, large as the moon in your eyes. Gentle like the snowflakes passing through, meeker than a rose waiting on you. Humble like the raindrops watering the earth, cool as an iceberg melting in time, larger than the sphinx guarding your life. Long as the Nile River flowing through your veins, stronger than the pyramids standing in the sand. Tall as Mount Everest, reaching the sky, lighter than a feather slumbering in the balances. Colorful like a rainbow to your spirit, giving hope to your soul. Free as a dove seated in a tree, lonelier than the dust waiting on we. I wonder if you can feel me!

DEAR AMERICA

I've seen your mansions and hibernated in your shacks, passed by mountains looking for tracks and watched both oceans run to the shores. I've come across many doors that were closed, passing by window from times of old, seeing souls that I wish I could hold, trying to open to open doors that were once closed. Passing through time trying to find something to hold after, crossing all these bridges on their shores, you learn from things that were cold, hoping to find someone to help rest your soul. Still following the stars by night, hoping they are leading me on a path that's light. After putting all my dreams in a heart, and then, borrowing a few from tomorrow. There isn't much bread falling from the sky, and my stomach has begun to cry. There won't be another slave ship coming by, only all the clouds from their jail cell passing by. As time goes by living in a lie.

AUTHENTIC LOVE

Sewn together by the heart of the creator born beyond the star in a paradise where there is no harm. It's like the snow it covers your life, then melts into your soul for times of old. Dreams often look for it, the wind is the only one that knows where it hibernates and waits. Flowers are authentic love best friend they are dressed and scented by the same spirit that has no end. Mortals try to purchase it with diamonds and gold along with promises they can never hold.

MY LOVING WIFE SHEILA

The candle lighting my life along this path with Christ, hand-in-hand we have never thought twice. Being blessed to have found each other under this beautiful blue sky, I thank God that you are my wife. I still remember our wedding day in Glencairn Garden, as if it was yesterday. Sheila you have brought so much joy into my soul giving me three beautiful flowers blooming in our sight. B.J. the son that warms my world with his charming smile of gold. Then Jeremy appears into our lives with eyes like the stars that light up the night. God has truly completed our life giving us one of his angels, Marisa to watch over our lives with her love and wonderful spirit that continues to blossom.

LOVE

Loves stronger than time, warm as the sun, cool like the wind in a storm, it can find you without following the stars; all that it needs is your hearts. Calmer than the sea, soft as a cloud, gentle as an infant slumbering in its mother's arm. Love stays away from temptation and is smarter than sin; it was born in the Garden of Eden and has no end. Love has no. foe and it will always flow, all that it needs is fertile hearts with meek minds. A tsunami can't drown love, fire can't harm it, hands can't hold it snow can't cover it only spirits can know it.

Love lays down to sleep with you each night and rises in your smile every morning. Love has no· address and it keeps no records, but it has a voice that only the soul can hear. Purer than a flower, quiet as the twinkling of an eye, faster than a shooting star on a moonless night. Sweeter than honey to the taste and remember love's never late.

GANG MEMBERS

Open your red and blue hearts. North America is carrying enough scars. Loved ones' voices litter the landscapes of time. Tombstones are the reminders. Death continues to prosper across the continent broken spirits are responsible. The republic that we hibernate in has failed. Tattoos and sign languages can tell. Mothers' tears fall like rain, addiction decorates the plains, castles of concrete and steel receive all of the hopeless. Time only know if the Western hemisphere will be healed.

50TH WEDDING ANNIVERSARY
ISAAC B SMITH AND GERALDINE SMITH

We continue to watch the sun smiling in the east each morning and close its eye in the west to rest. And walk hand in hand with the four seasons. Spring birds singing and building their homes in trees. Their offspring will soon be here. Our hearts have never been nearer. Summer flowers decorate the landscape, the wind can't wait to blow the fragrance throughout our days.

Autumn shows up painting the leaves on the trees from green to burnt orange. Time was tagging along and turned our hair from black to white. What a beautiful sight. Winter came by with all of its gifts. Snow leaving the sky to visit us here. Christmas bringing joy to all that can hear. Our love will endure forever. There is no fear.

IF I LEAVE YOU LORD

Where am I going to inhale that you haven't existed? You were here before the sun was born and even commanded the earth to be formed. Your eyes twinkled in the night when there were no stars to guide hearts.

To speak to the wind and it even obeys, surely you are the only way. Your sermon on the mount is truly the best advice that humanity could follow. The love and grace that you have shown me has transformed my life from misery after my spirit made its mind up to follow thee.

DON'T PLANT ME IN AMERICA

The sun is resigning and the moon's right behind him, stars are shooting every night. The wind finally asks why, a puppet rules the empire every forty-eight hours. Capitalism owns the tomorrows, destitute voices crying out in the wilderness.

Concrete jungles are what they hibernate in, predators decorate their days plagues are there to stay. The river of addiction flows free incarceration, gave their seeds a new birthday out of state. The fortresses that investors have designed collect generations of minds. Because they are blind all of their hope expired in the sixties two prophets that they didn't want them to follow. Out of a life, filled with emptiness on a continent where the souls will never prosper.

PASTOR MARY R. CROSBY

Eyes of light, voice of thunder, heart of gold, soul of love, spirit filled with beauty, will of stone, and wisdom from above. A life of faith and living example walking in our midst giving love and care to everyone that visits her existence. A fountain of life. The star twinkling in my sky with angel arms that held me tightly when my life wasn't so bright. When I needed someone to lift me up, you were there with a heavenly touch. You never wavered in your thoughts or even considered my faults. I sure appreciate your warm words and spiritual guidance that means so much. You have truly been a blessing to my sight.

CLEOPATRA

My wish is to watch the sunrise bloom in your eyes, and to feel the waves of love wash up on the shores, of my heart. As the four winds of time, carry our passion for all eternity; now that you have open the door to your soul, and allowed me to enter. Your sweet voice whispered the words that my existence has always wanted to feel. While your gentle arm reaches out pulling me near, letting me know that there is only love here. Time has joined us together, like the moon and stars in the night sky. Your love has strengthened, my life, and taken away all, the whys.

BEAUTY

Tall as the wind, wider than the sky, brighter than a star twinkling in the night; stiller than the moon on a homeless life. Fingerprints dancing in the minds of time, tomorrow's wonders, today's eyes, and prophecies being fulfilled, while the creator looks on and smile. Marvel if you must, but remember, appearances are only flesh deep, the hearts a lot farther just wait and see.

MOTHER

The leaves have turned from green to red and yellow again, and the sky is pink and blue. The wind is blowing cool air, I am just sitting here thinking of you.

I've never really got to know any of you because of the things we went through. The burdens that I carried as a child, was too much to get through. Trying to run away but never finding truth. Time and death have taken us apart and I still don't have a clue.

I am going to get on my knees and pray to God, you showed me to. Maybe he can wipe away a scar or two, after he has taken a walk through. I don't blame Dad anymore because I know the things he threw in this culture just trying to be true!

TEREISA

Tereisa, I just woke up and received a telephone call this morning the voice on the other end said that you were gone.

So I ask for your new address or phone number where I could reach you, when I need a shoulder to lean on.

Then they told me that you had passed on and that there was no address to where you had gone.

It makes my eyes flow water to know that a wonderful person like you had expired.

So I am going to write you a letter and mail it to God because, I know that's where you are, because he probably needs another Angel to help watch over the Earth.

And each night that I look out my window at the twinkling stars, I will always wonder how you are.

Tereisa, even though we are separated by eternity for now, I will always carry you in my mind and heart.

Rest now, your pure soul in the creator's arms and may you lovely smile continue warming the Earth.

Your Friend for Eternity,
Juan

JASMINE

Your smile warms the earth; your laughter is music in the wind; your caring spirit has no end. You are the most beautiful flower planted in God's garden of life, growing underneath this blue sky, sparkling like the stars in your mother's eyes.

I wish that I was there to be your umbrella when it's raining your coat, when you are cold, your protector while growing old.

You are the most wonderful daughter a father can have, so always be strong and carry a smile. If you ever get lonely deep down in your heart late at night, while laying in the dark, look out of your window at the stars and you will know that I am not very far from where you are.

Remember, I am never slumbering and never asleep, just always watching my lovely daughter smiling underneath these cirrus clouds; waiting to see all the beautiful things she is to bloom to be.

TO MY GRANDDAUGHTER MIA

Mia you are the lily growing in my life and the sun that lights my day, as I see you blossom each day.

When my eyes first touched you, my spirit feel safe with joy, knowing that time had placed you in my heart.

Your tiny eyes do not stare into the heavens with love and care, accompanied by your rosie cheeks that carries a smile that the world would soon see.

Mia you are a blessing in our family's lives and it's a joy to have a star like you twinkling in our sky and the moon is over there looming because he knows why, after watching so much love pass by.

Love Ana

LETTER TO MICHAEL
6/15/2001

Death comes by and you never understand why, but it always leaves you crying and standing around wondering why.

Can it teach me about tomorrow and take away all this pain and sorry.

I remember seeing you smiling and laughing, while we were playing marbles and then watching you play football at the fire station on Cherry Road, seeing you kickoff and the ball going into the road.

I am sorry that you were born to someone that didn't know how to love. But never forget that, I loved you, you need so much but, I was only a child and didn't have the touch.

Born in the sixties we didn't have much, but, I hold you in my heart missing your touch and even though you aren't here anymore Michael, I love you that much more.

I will never forget you and to let you know Bobby missing you as much and you probably already know that he has a little girl that, I have nicknamed Butterfly.

Tell Terry and Grandmama that, I said hi and that, I love you all.

NATIVE
9/7/20002

My hunting grounds are barren my teardrops are like spring rains, there's no one to know my pain.

My homeland flows with the blood of the innocent, before the Conquistadors appeared we use to grow in the wind, now we are in a spider's web and humanity isn't here they thirst for the yellow metal that lays between the blades of grass.

My mountains have been made low and my horizon's vanished the sun drifted away, my stars have fallen from my eyes and the moon refuses to show, our time has passed.

Will anyone ever know?

The love that, I had for these shores.

IN MEMORY OF MICHAEL PERNELL SMITH

Michael since you fell asleep my days aren't so bright it's like my sun has lost some of its light and the sky today is Carolina blue the November winds have begun to show.

I am just sitting here with my watery eyes thinking of you, my son and how the four winds of life toss you and how much I miss you.

Last night after church, I was standing outside looking at the moon and stars and wondered how you are.

But then, I remembered years ago, I placed you in God's hands and I know what he can do, Michael rest now your thirsty soul upon the creator's bosom where you won't thirst anymore.

Tell him of all the burdens that are carried by the wandering souls that can only see in the flesh and in him they can rest.

Michael my son, I know you have found joy in paradise, where there is no more pain and suffering only love and the sunlight to shine upon your pure soul.

Your loving Mother
Mrs. Geraldine Smith

Dear Grandmamma
A Tribute to Mrs. Lucille Collins

They told me that you are far beyond the stars, but you know that I will always wonder how you are. Little old lady with a pretty smile whose silky black hair time has painted gray; you took eight souls from nights they didn't need to know, from a cold North Carolina door, giving them love so they may grow, and you are sure appreciated.

Dear grandmamma, the cold winds have begun to show, and you are not here to know! You told me if I ever got lonely deep down in my heart, late at night, while laying in the dark, just look out my window at the Moon and stars and I would know that I wasn't very far from where you are.

I remember when they laid you down to rest in your Sunday's best, you may not have had any water to drink of air to breathe and the sun may not shine upon your lovely face, but in your dreams remember me this way, loving you each day.

Dear grandmamma, I've looked beyond the stars and finally found peace in my heart.

Gunshot House

Pear tree in the yard, rosebush beside the porch, little three-room shack, sitting on dust. Grandmamma sitting in her rocking chair, dipping her peach snuff, Michael lying on the bed not crying that much. Mama in the tiny kitchen making bread, the days are warm, and the nights are cold, so junior and I know what to do right out back beside the shack, there's a bag of coals and some needs to be brought into the shack.

The coal heater sits in the middle of the room, one bed on each side facing the door. There's one window facing the North, not much of a view, there's another gunshot house beside you, with a tin roof.

Each morning when you get out of bed make sure you put on your only shoes or you may pick up a splinter or two. It's very cold this morning but I know what to do, the little coal heater just needs a few maybe a branch or two. Mama needs some hot water it will take a few minutes, she just puts a pot of water on top of the coal heater soon it will be ready.

Struggling I the sixties, there's not much to do, the wind begins to show, rain clouds passing through hope that it doesn't rain too hard, the outhouse may over flood too.

9 Years Old
Dear God
6/30/02

I am nine years old and I've been told that you care very much about my soul, but did you know that it is torn?

Where, I live at its very cold and people have been sold. Maybe, I should mention, my name, but mama told me you already know everything.

But if you could, I sure wish you would help our family, because we are very poor, and my dad comes home drunk off Moonshine and abuses us mentally and physically you know.

I often get down on my knees and pray to you, like mama told me to, talking to you about her being disabled and how much it hurts her, we don't have a father to love us. Christmas is just another day.

And he has never even said happy birthday to any of us. I used to ask him for a quarter, but he told me to go to work for it so, I don't ask him for anything anymore.

Dear God, I often wonder if you can hear me, because nothing has changed it doesn't matter about me, but could you please stop mama's pain?

Change
8/5/03

Hair turning gray of living this way teeth rotting and walking on a cane living on borrowed time hoping that isn't in vain.

While standing at the great register of life waiting to get change the gentleman with the hair like wool and hands of brass quietly ask me, what I would, like to get change for.

As I reach into the earth and pull out my hand the gentleman quietly said, oh it's for the sea and then in a caring way he asks how would you like it and I began to speak, let the water recede back and the land come forth, there is a great multitude that need to come forth.

Then he began to speak with me in a humane way letting me know that he had changed it that way.

But he said that he could reach into the universe and pull out a planet and said it will be better to start a new humanity.

SNIPER

Free of a conscience guardian of the constitution on a mission of no return to show us how much I love red roses, white clouds and a blue sea. Turning into a ghost, the wind can't even see me. Stars follow me on my way to destiny, laying in silence for days waiting on a shadow. Breathtaking instrument attached to my fingertip. Leopold scope helps me see clearly. One strike is all I get. Then, I must vanish like a vapor back into the atmosphere carrying with me memories of my tour.

My Teacher
Mrs. Caldwell

She gathers us under her wings like a mother hen teaching her subjects that have no ends. Silky white hair tossed by the wind, caring blue eyes that want me to succeed. Carrying a charming smile and a lovely voice that is a friend to a multitude of souls that have blossomed from her existence, encouraging hearts that have doubts about exams that can change their paths. The attentiveness that she has shown my spirit is a blessing to my life and I sure appreciate it.

ILLEGITIMATE

Two illegitimate seeds blooming on the continent and another never grew without a protector to see it through. He's trying to run away from a feeling he never knew. Now he has two flowers growing in two different gardens without a gardener to brighten their way, a cycle that has been going on for decades. The protector having deep scars in his mind that will never heal because of the love he was never able to feel in this culture that steals. The little flowers are the only losers. They grow up to be like you.

CHRISTALYN

All of life's cares have washed away from my eyes it's been half a century on this odyssey for endless love. I often hear the wind whispering words that my spirit yearns to feel, not knowing that you were so near. Now, I know what it means to find your soulmate in the Milky Way, even when, I don't see you, I can still feel you. The spiritual love that you have brought into my life has helped me grow and I can never let you go. The sound of your celestial voice has charmed my heart on this journey called life with words that can only be shared in the dark. Your smile warms my life and those diamond eyes have me hypnotized.

KIKI

You are the most beautiful flower blooming in the Milky Way. An angel sent by God to heal my broken heart. My daughter, as you continue to bloom in this garden of life, always carry a smile and think nice. Because clouds come in all different shapes and sizes, rain comes often, but don't let that bother you. Take a look around it helps everything become new. Kiki keep following the stars that are in your heart. They will lead you to the treasure that's waiting on you. I am proud of the princess that you have grown to be and that you are blooming in my mist, I love you.

REAL LOVE

It can't be found. It comes without a sound. The wind doesn't know where it lives. The sun has warmed hearts for millions of years, but Love makes it feel. Currency can't possess it, minds thirst for its companionship before they expire. The soul will know when it knocks on its door carrying Lyrics that last for eternity. Two hearts sewn together walking across the stars searching for another galaxy where they could be alone. To melt into each other's eyes under the moonlight, while whispering words that can only be shared at night.

Born Free
12/20/02

Like the wind that blows through the earth's door, free like the sun that rises in men's eyes.

Like a shadow, free as the eagle's soars across the evening sky, as time goes by.

Free like the stars shooting across a dark sky, as the moon sits by.

Free like the clouds rolling by, free as the love in a new mother's eyes, as the newborn cries.

Free like the snowcap mountain waiting for the sunlight that shines so bright.

Free as the blood that flows through your veins like rivers of change.

Free like the fish in the sea, as a bird sitting in a tree.

Free like the thoughts that flow through my mind that you can't see for all the little children that will never be free, that you can't see!

Free like the fingerprints dancing in the winds of time like the light that shines from the east that has no end.

Free as the day, free like the night that rests in the west.

Sons of Men

O, sons of men you have fallen farther than a falling star and your lights burned out faster than a shooting star.

Passing by eagle's eye, you turned away from being your brother's keeper to putting stumbling blocks in front of other people.

Only to place their fallen seeds into castles of steel, never to heal.

The webs that you have been spun even pierce the only begotten Son.

How long must we mourn?

Is sleep the only freedom that we will ever know?

Grandma
12/24/02

I can still hear your voice speaking of times that weren't so kind, back in the North Carolina town.

Where you took the burdens of so many upon yourself, the love you show the broken lives you encounter was tremendous.

You were the most loving person that I would ever have in my life.

The love you show me as a child still warms my life today; I will carry you in my heart each day that I breathe.

I wish that you were here because my sky is cloudy, and my days cold, now that I am growing old!

Grandma we have fallen on stony grounds now and Michael couldn't take all the frowns.

His heart's broken, and his dreams were gone; he couldn't take this gruel world anymore, now he passed on.

My Shepherd
6/19/03

I often daydream about the first time my eyes touch you, as if the creator let you walk right out of paradise, glowing as the sun.

Knowing that one of his sheep had gone astray, I even moved a chance in and tried to take the picture of you out of my heart.

I told it to faith, but I had back slide along the way.

I was thinking about today, I have been so long this way and you love me anyway.

I haven't shown you my best way, but I've even gotten down on my knees and told the creator what holds my heart in the wishing well.

About giving my love to you to put in your soul and keep it warm, because it has crossed too many great gulfs alone.

He lets me hibernate and rises me up before it's too late, sending you out of the clouds to help show me the way to a better time and space.

If not for you, not for a single one of my dreams would have ever came true, my lover and my Shepard.

And if I should lay down to rest and my eyes don't see you anymore remember me, in your dreams and know that, I loved you.

Karl
9/18/2003

Rest now your beautiful soul upon the creator's bosom where your watery eyes can be dried from your tiring labor underneath this blue sky.

Tell him of the yokes that are carried by many souls whose eyes can see only in the flesh and in him they can only find rest.

Karl my friend walks in the sunlight for all eternity and I hope that you have found peace in the land where there is no darkness only love and the sunlight to shine upon your charming smile.

Abby
9/2/03

Sweet and classy light blue eyes piercing through the galaxies as you tiptoe across the stars you have found your way too many hearts.

The same way an angel plays the harp, leaving your beautiful smile across the universe, like roses growing upon the Earth.

Your loving spirit has no end like the sun that smiles in the East and takes its time, vanishing in the west. Abby hearing your voice is like hearing two love birds sing on a spring morning and your heart is larger than the sky and your love is going to reach farther than the wind, where your wonderful soul will have no omega.

If I Had a Home

I sure hope that it would be warm, free of storms, it doesn't have to have twenty-four doors only two, one for love the other for you, or twenty-five windows, just one that the sun smiles through.

It doesn't have to sit high on a ridge, just on a planet, where humanity can fill. There's no need for it to have enough bricks in it to build a pyramid, just enough to shelter me from the west sins.

It doesn't have to have enough light in it, to light the world, just the light of my life. The floors don't have to be waxed, just without tracks and the roofs really don't have to bee tin, just one that has end.

It doesn't have to have heat, just the rhythm of your heartbeat, and it really don't have to have running water, just the well that you drink from and you won't thirst anymore.

It doesn't have to have ten rooms, just one for me you.

Tear Drops
7/1/03

Just existing here wringing my eyes out thinking of you, I have already passed through two towels daydreaming of you.

My heart bleeds blue, the wave that sweeps me out to sea, just went away, leaving me to drift along the way.

Trying to put all of life cares in a bottle, will I ever have a cloudless tomorrow.

I am going to get down on my knees and tell it to my faith, maybe it will show me a star to lead my way.

Missing you gave me a feeling that I never knew.

The teardrops that flow down my face are warm, but have no form, my sun refuses to shine, since you aren't around.

My moon drifted away the night your heart went to stay, and the stars don't come out to play.

I wonder if the rain could take the place of the teardrops that roll down my face to give them a break.

Me
7/4/01

I have sat and watched all of your great wonders and have heard you thunder and seen the lighting flash flood, across the sky and witness the snow blowing by and even seen stars fall from the sky and I have to not once asked you why.

Sitting here watching the sunset in the sky, and wondering why my Twin, brother had to expire.

What a great purpose it must had to be for you to take him away from me.

Leaving me to walk through this world of uncertainty and to live life never to be free,

I thank thee for taking my twin brother, it makes my heart sing knowing that he didn't have to live in someone else's dreams.

Cotton Fields

Old cotton field will you ever heal from all the souls you help seal, soaking in so much blood from so many bruised heels, never thinking that they may fill.

Crossing so many hills after sailing hundreds of years on many tears, the wind carries their voices through time and past time, but they will never since even your seeds can't fill the timeless heartaches of their fears.

Why has fate dealt them so many itching ears, crawling up and down cotton rows, pulling the Cotton sacks hoping that the clouds would come shade the sun and weep, to cool their parching tongues.

Dear Brother, Isaac B Smith

We have faced the festering era of racism and drank from the colored streams of time, segregation often came out to play with us in our cold South Carolina town all of our stars fell in the sixties. The writers of discontent always visited the gunshot house that we hibernated in.

Dear Mama, bless her heart, she never had a start underneath these red, white, and blue stars; disabled and stranded on hopelessness she couldn't see. Then integration found its' way to you and I. After going to the back doors for so many years, we began school in the Caucasian will!

Dear Brother, we have faced the cruelest times that can be a phantom, never having a protection to guide us like the stars, when the stumbling blocks found our lives. We are truly each other's keeper.

Born in Captivity

Little black boy with his washed-out dreams wondering if he could possibly be taken out of this stream. His lightless eyes have, begun to see, his ghetto word of few possibilities.

His elementary school has become juvenile hall and the college his friends attend is state prison for higher learning.

The old folks home where he visits is the federal penitentiary.

Now let's take a look at their past, they never had a country, now that's sad, their names was never last.

He began running with the things in the night trying to find some light.

But the only thing that he found was some things that would one day take his life.

And all he said was, dear mama, you gave me breath knowing that I would die; now you just sit and weep and cry as they carry me by.

People standing around asking why as they drive me by, but don't cry, remembering that I was born to expire.

So please part with the water in your eyes we won't have these tears on the other side.

Nubians

Where have you gone after being so pure your fingerprints still cover the earth floor, but things have turned to the worst since your birth.

The winds carried a lot of your seeds to the west in the belly of ships laying shackled side by side counting three four hundred at a time.

When turning over turning over someone else.

After landing three months later to work the fields that will never heal or feel, looking at the stars in the night you learn your plight but, you would never be out of sight like a falling star to the earth leaving its home in the sky you have fallen in the west never to rest.

Being placed in slums that surely will cause you harm when they don't need you palms.

The pyramids that you once built in the land of Cush are still there, but you have vanished into this insanity!

Why
10/11/80

My America, I've watched you grow born in nineteen sixty, my twin brother and I, to parents that were very poor.

Reading in your history books about thing, that I wish I didn't know, not knowing that my twin would never grow.

Getting down on my knees praying to a God, wondering if he would ever show, hearing mama crying late at night through the bedroom door.

Laying there wondering if daddy loved us anymore being poor did little to help you know going uptown seeing the colored water fountains I didn't know that mother showing me to the backdoor. No smiling faces at the stores just someone looking as if they weren't sure.

When we left home I had just finished plating grandma's silky gray hair while she sat on the front porch in her rocking chair dipping her peach snuff.

Mothers were at the church next door playing the tambourines, sister Mary's speaking in tongues, I wonder if they know what it means.

The rain drops begun to fall from the sky hope they are clean because ever since we moved beside this pool room I have become unclean if you know what I mean.

Pops out back working on that old sixty seven ford fair lane. He's a great mechanic considering the culture that he was born in didn't' permit him to learn to read or write.

He could pick a cotton seed and plow a field and that's after the wheel.

I
8/4/03

I wish I was a smile, because I love seeing them come around, I wish that I was a cloud to shade you from times doubts. I wonder if I was a tear, could you hear me? I wish that, I oxygen then you would need me.

I wish I was the wind, then I could speak to humanity about its' sins.

I wish that I was a physician so that, I could heal all mankind's illnesses. I wonder if heaven really has sixteen gates, because I can't find my way in yet.

I wish I was the sun so that I could warm society's heart. I wish that I was the moon then I wouldn't have to come out so soon. I wish that I was a shooting star then, I could give you the desires of your hearts.

I wonder if I was raindrops, could I help you grow. I wish that I was love then, I could give myself to all of you.

I wonder if I was a candle in the wind could you see me? I wish that I was the snow falling so that I could cover you from this culture abhors.

I wish that I was time, then I could barrow from mother earths beautiful mind when I return to the dust will you reminisce about me if I had the keys to heaven you could have them.

Passed Away
12/11/81

Living in Hades there wasn't much for you to do and for some reason crack cocaine found you if had nothing new to show you it only took the last of you.

I can still remember that cold November sunrise I was sitting in the deer stand facing the east as the sunlight began to peep through the first doors.

The wind carries your name, but I didn't harvest anything only to return home to find out that the creator had harvested you.

The maid at the motel said she knocked on the door a little after you were to vanish.

But there was no answer, so she entered the room and that's when she found you laying across the bed just taking a late snooze.

So she said to herself that I'll just return after I have cleaned my other rooms.

Only to return and find out that you had faced your last noon.

Your shell laying there without despair and without care.

Stephanie

To wish on a star was not the reason I chose you, to hope on a shooting star could not hold you, the twinkle in your eyes lets me know that I should do whatever is in my power to love you.

Your smile captured me as I was walking through life wishing to see the love that's waiting on me.

Your voice speaks the words that my heart has wanted to hear, and your arms reach our letting me know that there is nothing to fear.

Your steps move me to a place that I have never known a place called home.

Your heart has reached out to me leaving me speechless knowing the love you have for me, my Stephanie.

Lost Love

I can still hear the tears roaming down your face and dropping off the couch as you lay there weeping during the night.

Now wishing that I could rewind time wouldn't have been so blind. The stars that I had been following lead me to a tree that I started to eat from; the fruit was sweet at the time in my mouth but after swallowing became bitter in my stomach

Now searching just to see your shadow while waiting across the Milky Way had you simply fallen out of my pocket and blown away in the wind, if that was my only sin my tears cry out for you in my dreams.

Now I know it's the end.

Alexandria's Smile

To my daughter Alex with her cherry smile thin as a rail and feel with lives cares. The first time I saw you we were in a South Carolina town your tiny life has taken you all around.

Flying high above the clouds your sparkling eyes do stare waiting to land at the airport who would be there? Time will take your beautiful life thousands of miles and I am always happy to see your pretty smile come around.

Your bushy eyebrows paint your face two ponytails help lead your way going through life always carry a smile and remember I love having you around.

Even though I am not there, always be meek knowing that I am carrying you inside my heart, so be sweet.

Me and You
8/30/01

It's the same sky that the slaves looked at when brought up from below and maybe not seen anymore.

It's the same ocean that carried you from everything that you would ever know.

They are the same clouds that hasn't turned out so proud. It's the same wind that blows through your hair where there is no end.

It's the same sun that warms you when your heart is cold it's the same moon that lets you know that it's time to change.

They are the same stars that wonder where you are and it's the same snow that covers the earth's floor.

This is the same water that you drink and won't thirst anymore, it's the same dirt that is going to lead us into eternity, you know.

THE CORNERS

Where dreams are washed away into the drains of time; eyes very rarely see the sun smile. Street pharmacists hang around, peddling poison to the zombies that have lost their way underneath these red, white, and blue stars! The moon weeps for their spirits leaving a clear view of the sin blooming in the midst. The corners a breeding ground for the hopeless, a robber of souls even the seeds blooming in the wombs are casualties. The castles of steel litter the landscapes of time filled with wretched souls that will never be held, only growing cold in these times of old! **It's** strange how time has turned them to stones on the corners, glass pipes litter the blocks, exterminating the lives of the hopeless. I've seen so much dirt done on these sad corners it makes my heart wonder if heaven has a ghetto.

LISTEN

Before my existence has expired, I would like mankind to know how, I feel. It makes my heart weep to continue observing humanity race down the tracks of time in ignorance. Mankind has not learned anything from the past, nations have been destroyed and generations birth into slavery. Names lost forever and the only witness to their breath is the sun and moon, they heard them asking the creator why. The dust is going to welcome all mortals after this temporary journey.

Utopia

The earth is so beautiful from looking down from the sky it makes you wonder why we must all expire. I've lived through the sins and plagues under these white fluffy clouds and witnessed the destruction of humanity; and at last, I have found a home above the clouds where it is warm.

There's no hate in any form only my love and heaven to roam. There's no tears to run because your eyes will never see harm. No color to make you feel along. No names that can cause you any harm, no currency to put you in a class and no symbols to help remember past.

Only stars to light your path.

BORN

To a mom and pop that are illiterate, on a vile South Carolina plantation. Where they are voiceless and hopelessness lives in their eyes. The cotton field is waiting every morning before the sunrise and there is nowhere to hide, two broken souls that must fill the cotton sacks until they are overflowing.

If they are not, there will be a lashing showing, from the cow skin whip. The scorching sun is no one's friend, even the tears that stream down their face are hot. So many wasted thoughts, two brothers sold off the auction blocks. Slavers from Georgia, need to add to their stock, two spirits never having a choice. Woe to me, given sight in this sea of bondage. Where God will never hear or see me hibernating in squalor, this is my tomorrow.

Children of War

How many they be more than me flying high above the clouds to bring only death and destruction to us?

There are millions of dollars spent ton harming see and all it takes is a little love for me, but you still can't see the love inside of me?

The bombs fall to the earth so endlessly, how much can she take before it's the end of us?

I wonder if what we have means so much to thee that you would take my life to see, and after that would it satisfy thee?

Dear mama, can we be recaptured from our adversaries, insanity of a life committed to uncare and extinguish the tears and remove the terror of the brutal day and endless nights sure to be reborn.

LIFE

Mysterious like ideology waiting on you and me with arms stretched out for all to see. Gentler than a newborn baby in its mother's dreams. Softer than a nimbus cloud surrounding eternity. Older than tears that run through veins. Lonely like an eagle riding the winds of time. Life is sweeter than a honeycomb is to the taste. Quieter than a comet fleeing the universe. Bright as a star twinkling in the night. Stronger than death that no one wants to feel, not knowing that there is nothing to fear. Hotter than a volcano that erupts every century, thirstier than a camel that thinks it sees a mirage. Life is longer than the breath that you own. Faster than a heartbeat that has no home. Life loves to see us reborn.

SLAVE CHILDREN

Have you ever heard of the roses that grew out of slavery in this Red, White and Blue soil? Their victimized eyes will never have a mother's love to shine in their lives and the thirst for her touch can never by quench. As they lay slumbering and asleep on the cabin's cold dirt floor, the moonlight peeps through the door, stars don't want to know. Swaddling cloths paint their bodies. Bare feet often follow the centuries of shame without names. No fathers to protect them from tomorrow's sorrows in the cotton fields that can never hear. Their journeys often began at the auction blocks filled with raindrops falling from their hearts while humanity stands by and watches.

AUSCHWITZ

A name that time is ashamed of. Letters that spell its name wish that they were never born. The sun asks the Creator if it has to shine upon its face. Six sets of railroad tracks run through your veins carrying passengers to their shame arriving around the clock.

1941 would get to watch. Auschwitz would be the final stop underneath a Poland sky that couldn't hear cries. Cries that still reach through time from the multitude of souls inside of the four breathtaking chambers that words could never hold. The water out of their eyes would give them their only showers. Wooden bowls lead them to the starvation hours. Hearts beating in time remembering ancestors' faith and loving smiles that have helped build a nation that's proud.

BOB MARLEY

A revolutionary, whose voice is stronger than the wind and his dreadlocks have no end, thin fingertips walking up and the acoustic guitar charming the voiceless with metaphors of freedom and spirituality. I heard him reminiscing about the buffalo soldiers that were stolen from Africa. The clouds are distributing his lyrics around the Milky Way echoing, minds wake up to unity. Stand up at the table of humanity were one love lives before memories keep killing. Don't let a constitution buy your soul, teardrops are falling all around the shores. The hydrogen bomb knows no love and an assassin's bullet couldn't steal his spirit, on his odyssey to unlock the mind of the oppressors, because their eyes can't feel. Heartbeats are trying to run away but never getting far drowning underneath, this ocean of stars.

MY WILL

I leave my love to the Dear poor children of the globe and my feelings are to be distributed by the wind, so that humanity can begin again. Give my ashes to the ocean it knows all my ancestors and my mind to the leaders of mankind because they are blind. My eyes give them to the tomorrows so that, I can see if there are still ghettos. I leave my ears to all the voices that paint the landscapes of time that will never be felt.

Please take my heart to the castles of concrete and steel to where the felons and outcast suffer that will never heal. Plant my hands with flowers, I never want to stop giving love and condolences, place my feet on a shooting star so that they can find freedom for us all. Take my voice to the sun maybe it can help all souls that have been done harm, tell the moon not to mourn.

Geronimo
8/29/03

I can still hear your spirit crying out in the wilderness to be free and to walk hand in hand with dignity. Your pain and great loss hasn't been in vein, the wind carries your name through time and it will always shine like the sun that rises in the east and sleep in the west where your thirst could never rest.

They wanted your soul, but it has already grown old and it belongs to the wind.

Riding north, south, east, and west in this wonderland of injustice, if your visions were a dream or a nightmare at least could your god give your people a nest, they have no rest spirits tired and stomachs crying for something else.

Born of the sun and wean by the Moon, time was the only thing to consume you.

The stars lead your eyes astray knowing they had witness better days, no reservations to cloud your ways.

You and your people, tried to run away but never getting far, trapped underneath all these stars.

Exterminated now and gone from humanity forever, apaches rest your worried souls and it's my wish upon a star, that you have found freedom in the happy land, that you once knew.

CRACK BABIES

Hush little butterflies don't you cry the creator is going to dry your watery eyes, he knows that there is a thorn in your lives. You may never have a mama in your eyes, so always walk with your head up high, underneath this Red, White, and Blue sky. Time has dealt you a bitter hand in this land of ends; it's hard to understand the four winds, knowing that none of your beautiful flowers have ever sinned. Seizures and withdraws paint your day, medications lay in the way, love very rarely comes out to play. Addiction doesn't have to be in our lives to say, the sun is going to smile each day and the stars are in the night sky to help guide your way. It's beyond comprehension that you beautiful butterflies are born with this sorrow.

DEAD

Gardens of stones continue to bloom in the Milky Way. Each continent is littered with nuclear waste. Warfare is flourishing in the middle east, helping eyes to rain on the western hemisphere, Mother earth spread her arms and accepts all the expired minds.

Knowing that there is a multitude standing in line, waiting to follow the blind. The sun wishes that he had somewhere to hide from the deity that is soon to arrive. While the moon just wants to take a ride, to where love resides. Because it has vanished from the bloodstream of humanity, allowing dead to be proud.

Feelings

I wish that I was a creator so that I could reach inside of man's heart and maybe wipe away a few scars, clearing the way for a new start. Putting you to sleep isn't hard, waking you up has become the part. Creation has to have a new start, because hate lives inside of many hearts.

O, time, you must know, it's hard when there is so much love in my heart, looking at history from the dark, my brown eyes have begun to sob, if only the water out of our eyes we could drink, maybe humanity wouldn't sink.

Born, North, South, East, and West, in this great universe of unrest. If only this was really a dream or a nightmare at best, could time stop for a second and give the world a rest? There is no place to take the less, even Jesus came by and couldn't find a nest.

If only this was a test, I would give my life so that humanity could rest. Move the throne from under your vest and give the mother a rest. Born of a woman like all the rest, let's take the time and reach inside and bring out the best.

AFRICA

To the homeland of my ancestors it makes my heart weep to see you that way even though I am thousands of miles away, because the four winds carried me four hundred years to this day. You don't even have enough food for today but have the military ability to annihilate your entire race. I've seen the mask grave that runs through your time, now, I feel your pain and suffering each seconds of my time. Gold and oil lay in your diamonds sparkles in your eyes today. Diseases planted there to stay death often comes out to play. If only the tears out of the deceased eyes we could drink maybe, Africa would sink, I wonder, what will happen to the millions of soul's unfulfilled dreams. To my heavenly father that lives on high, yes, the one with the all seeing eye, when these wandering souls return to you broken and tired will you please lay them down somewhere that's quiet.

DEAREST MAMA

Time gave you a bitter well to drink from in this climate of discontent, and your first steps on this continent were on a plantation. Carrying water up and down rows in the cotton fields that can never hear or feel, your five year old footprints paint the way to shame. Your innocent spirit never knew a paternal, mother or fathers charm their hearts, felt too much harm. The tiny brown eyes, that you have meets the sun rise each morning from where it hides. On your mule and wagon ride to where souls have expired. Dearest Mama your adolescent years were spent reminiscing, about the cotton fields and holding your younger sibling tight, during the curse nights. The dreams, she had inside the one room cabin that leans on dirt is to have someone to adore. Clouds often visit but the only raindrops that are falling is from her eyes, they have nowhere else to hide they must escape from your inside. The secrets that she has locked in time, often runs from the sunshine they would rather live in darkness until the end of time.

REGRETVILLE

You can't follow the stars, because they don't know the way. Even the wind has nothing to say, a comet passed by it one day fleeing the Milky Way. The sun refuses to come out and play, the clouds are the only transportation around they circle the mind. Regretville the keeper of the soul's anguish neighbor to hades, rain comes by to help hide my tears. Sometimes, I wonder if heaven will be a waste of time. Seeing faces ending in the wind, while I keep running back to yesterday's voices and dream catchers. Sitting here holding my breath reminiscing about past transgressions only helps, living in regret prosper; leaving me without a tomorrow.

DEAR GOD

When you lay me down to sleep please consider the things you will for me then judge. Allowing me to be born Negro in poverty underneath a hopeless sky knowing that, I would never be free. Suffering as an adolescent in a shack on Fewell St. with a queen that has been disabled since giving breath to us. My twin brother would never be, health care couldn't see and to a broken father who is always bitter from being planted in a culture of racism. Whose father was found slain on the side of a cold dirt road only nineteen fifty two would know who took his breath. Dear God, how am, I going to survive with all the fruit from my family tree expiring and my eyes have never got to see them speak.

Born a have not, cultivated in a climate of discontent, all of my dreams spoiled right before me. If it is possible that, I may live again could you please let me be born in a galaxy where there is no dieter, currency, color or sin.

If I Could
10/17/02

I would take the pain away and give you a brighter day, so that the thorns wouldn't be in your hearts to stay.

If I could have given life to you in another world, I would have, and the water that flows down your cheeks like rivers, I would dry up like a desert, if only I knew how.

The bridges that separate you from all other nationalities, I would bill back, if had the material.

And all your seed that have been carried away by the four winds, if I could take them out of other pockets, I would take them back home and paint them by the still waters, where they may have a tomorrow.

THE FUTURE

Wars continue to bloom in the Middle East oil hibernates underneath. Dictators are leading spirits astray martyrs are here to stay, covetousness often comes out to take. Nuclear weapons know where we eat; ideology has made humanity weak, by dividing blind minds even farther from the true meaning of creation. Refugees are fleeing the nations' casualties have begun to multiply in the wind, voices come in many shapes but there's no time to taste. Because another deity wants to make a dialect extinct on this planet of abhor. Remember love holds the keys to life; hieroglyphs paint our souls and eyes.

SLEEP

Keeper of my eternal soul, freeing me from this immoral and sinful world. Hold me close in your bosom so that I mayn't falter because my life here has been littered with regret and temptations. Time guides me as I walk down the hall of two truths where my heart will be weighed against a feather. Remember the icons my eyes were leading to see, shape in inequity following thirst that will never satisfy. We sleep the only peace that I will ever know. Thank you for all of the dreams that weren't cold, knowing that you were never my foe. I am yours, always to hold.

DEATH

Death so strong so proud you have nothing to fear but, I often wonder if you can hear or see the river of tears that are left here. Your grip has a hold no one can shake clear, runaway poor/folks even sleep with you there. Do you have any stars and a moon where you sleep, does the sun ever come out and warm the souls' fears or the rain come out to play, the snow can't even stop your day. Is there a ghetto where you hibernate to help abhor to continue to feel, do you ever get lonely late at night while lying there in the dark dreaming of another life that will never have apart. Death can, I come and visit you before I expire to make sure that, I will fit into your republic that exists beyond breath.

EBOLA

Why did you ride the clouds to a west African sky bringing with your regurgitation, diarrhea and hemorrhaging? You have brought rain from the eyes of many souls that will never be held. Quarantine waits in the days while death often comes out to stay. If I may inquire, where is your birth place? Never mind the date. Scientists would like to know where you hibernate. Physicians don't have time to play. A number of spirits each day are withering away and there aren't enough greenhouses for them to lay. A vaccine is a millennium away. Generations will never have anything to say; even the sun will never remember their days.

The wind carries name and shooting stars are the only ones to know their claims. After seven days of anguish, the dirt accepts the shadows.

LIVING A LIFE I DIDN'T CHOOSE

Conceived in a dimension of harm to mortals whose pigmentation classified them as less than human. Preventing them from prospering in the Milky Way. I couldn't reach and touch a star even with my thoughts. Dreams disappearing in my heart, can you wish upon a soul in a space where gravity waits? Fingerprints are out of date and unfaithfulness often comes out to play. Regret has moved in to stay, after trying to hold on to a spirit that only wants what the eyes thirst for.

Pure in heart trapped in an atmosphere where love don't exist stars runaway from a lonely midnight sky. Voices reach out to the wind wanting to know if the Creator can hear them wondering if the grave is the end.

DEATH ROW

Breathing here in this quiet storm twenty three seven, three sixty five listening to time in my five by nine. It seems like yesterday since, I lost my way, guiding myself to the injection table. Late at night, I can feel the water rising in my tear ducts on the way to overflowing, the dams of my eyes rushing down my cheeks. My meals are catered but that's not a treat. The light shines all night but gives no heat the cool wind shows twenty four seven and I can't sleep, you can even see through the blankets. My hammock is made of iron and bolted to the concrete floor with two inch plastic mattress and no pillow you know. The camole is stainless steel with the sink attached to it, that rest against the concrete wall with steel bars. This is my house and I hope you never visit it. I long to see the stars and to try to catch a fish before, I leave this beautiful world where, I cause so much grief.

ON MY DEATH BED

Remember that, I didn't choose to be born in captivity in the Milky way. Where, I am living out someone else's dreams. My mind is tired of being trapped under a constitution that's not for me. My eyes have witness an emperor slain, in longhorn territory, before he could put his autograph on a reparations law. That will help the children of slaves that were auctioned on these shores. That will never be able to open any economical doors as long as this republic is breathing. I have suffered under these stars with millions of other spirits, with my same D.N.A. knowing that we have no voice. Abolitionist has painted the landscapes of time with nouns and verbs only to be extinguished. I am expiring now and when, I see the creator. I will ask him, why he allowed our D.N.A. to be in servitude on a continent and abused forever.

MY BEST FRIEND PHILLIP MARSHALL

It's been thirty-five years that we have been riding in the chariot of life: eating off of the same plate and never thinking twice. A bond that's stronger than the steel that we were training with when we first met in the gym. I never knew how talented of a horticulturalist you were until I saw your garden: plants swaying in the wind. Oak Park Rd. leads the way to the castle of love where at times there were no vacancies. That's where I met a princess: your little sister whom I betrayed. We often spend days at the lakes together angling and at night throwing snow at the starlight.

I COULDN'T HAVE A WORSER FATHER

I don't mean to reminiscent about my father, but he was an abuser. His companion was moonshine and not the moonlight in the night. He never had any encouraging words to con, our storms in this sea of harm. I often get down on my knees, and ask my creator why was, I born to someone that is incapable of loving. Reared in poverty and stranded on hopelessness, I wonder if anyone cared. I couldn't have a worse father, a poor provider, but not by choice racism was the boss. He was conceived in the climate of illiteracy. Birth in abhor and weaned in the cotton fields now, I know why he can't feel.

I WISH THAT I WAS NEVER BORN

The Western Hemisphere is the stage, my creators are illiterate, and slavery made the choice. The only steps for me to follow leads to the cotton fields were spirits vanish in hopelessness. I told my dreams never to return, because I don't want them trapped inside a doomed vessel. The sunrise brings sorrow to my eyes, and the night introduced horror to my adolescent sister's body. Three decades have drifted away like cloud hurrying across the sky. I only pray for a pair of wings to take my mind to a universe that, conquers have never seen.

In case of my demise, put my flesh on top of a six feet wooden platform, and lite a fire underneath. Then smile for me, please give my ashes to the wind. I don't want them spread on this constitution continent were, even they will never be free.

About the Author

Jerry Smith a native of South Carolina. An athlete who played sports throughout school into his late twenties. His first job was at Catawba nuclear station. Smith also spent twenty years in the communications field and loved it. Smith current attends York Technical College.

"Poetry became a big part of my life more than twenty years ago and consumes and has consumed me ever since. To write something that encourages someone and bring love, light into the world that is my goal."

Made in the USA
Columbia, SC
01 April 2023

14632264R00159